High Way From Hell

Using **EMOTION**
to **FAN THE FIRE** *of*
ENLIGHTENMENT

Cover design by George Foster
Interior book design by www.KareenRoss.com

With commitment to our environment and out of respect for the
earth, this book is printed on archival quality, acid-free paper using
100% post-consumer recycled paper.

Printed in the United States of America.

ISBN 13: 978-0-9792797-0-6 ISBN 10: 0-9792797-0-4

If you are unable to obtain this book from your local bookseller
you may order it directly from the publisher. Quantity discounts
for organizations are available. Call toll free: 1-877-832-4400
or visit www.spiritwindpublishing.com

Published by Spirit Wind Publishing, Navarre, Florida

Publisher's Cataloging-in-Publication Data

White, Moonstone Star.
    High way from Hell : using emotion to fan the fire of enlightenment
/ by Moonstone Star White.
    p. cm.
    Includes bibliographical references and index.
    ISBN 978-0-9792797-0-6
1. Emotions. 2. Self-actualization (Psychology) 3. Spiritual life.
4. Subconsciousness. I. Title.

BF531 .W52 2007
152.422--dc22   2007901552

Disclaimer: This book is not for the faint-hearted. It is not for the victims of the world who want to blame others for their problems. The ideas presented are based on the author's experience. Your choice to consider or use the information is your own. By reading this book, you understand and agree that neither the author nor the publisher may be held liable for your results in the application or mis-application of the information presented. Taking responsibility for yourself is the first step toward emotional freedom!

This book is dedicated to Skip

*For the profoundness and depth to which you
have reached into my heart...for being my
perfect companion on our journey into Spirit...
for your unwavering acceptance of me as I am...
You know me as well as anyone
possibly could.*

Moonstone Star White

High Way From Hell

Using **EMOTION** to **FAN THE FIRE** of **ENLIGHTENMENT**

Spirit Wind Publishing
Navarre, Florida

TABLE OF CONTENTS

Table of Contents

The Wizard

I searched the world over
For something to call true.
For all my sorry searching
There was nothing I could do
To calm the raging waters
Wreaking havoc in my head.
I couldn't give up because after all,
Where would that have led?
I gazed at my reflection thinking
"Might as well be dead."
My life had become heavy
As solid yellow lead.
A wizard out of nowhere
Did suddenly appear;
He said "The magic lies within you.
Start your searching here."
I fought, I cried, I struggled,
I did not want to play.
I said "My life is nothing –
This cannot be the way."
The wizard stood there beaming,
His face a brilliant light.
I could not help believing
That maybe he was right.
Gradually the wizard's image
Began to disappear,
And I realized I was gazing
Into reflective mirror.
His voice barely whispered
As he finally was gone:
"I shall never leave you –
You and I are one."

—Moonstone Star White

The Gift

In the beginning there was the Void. Infinite and vast were the depths of its darkness. It was unknown, even to itself, because there was nothing created to realize it. It was a cosmic soup of un-manifest, limitless potential. Something stirred within the Void. Inspiration arose and the power to manifest sprang forth as divine force, an intention of The One. The Void, which contained all potential and yet nothing definable, was the resource for a staggering plethora of possibility. Universes were born and dimensions of existence were created. Rules of participation were engaged, such as the force of gravity, planetary orbit and atomic oscillation. The One became fascinated with and desired to experience everything it could imagine or create. The One set its creations free by endowing them with re-generating qualities and a gift called "free will". Little did The One realize how ungraciously the gift would be received...

*Life is the nature of spiritual
experience.*

*Fully realizing our spiritual
natures while incarnate –*

Now that is the challenge.

*When you remember your divine
nature,*

*Your joy at this remembrance is
God's joy.*

Welcome home.

1

Life is the Feeling of Spirit

Two thousand years ago an enlightened being who was ahead of his time said, "Seek first the Kingdom of Heaven and all else will be added to you." He added, "The Kingdom of Heaven is within you." The instructions were clear. That is where the search for Spirit must begin. At first it feels like uncharted terrain, a wilderness of emotions, judgments and resisted experiences. Let feeling be your guide as you navigate through life. Discover whatever you feel on the inside and embrace it. When you can do this you will know compassion for all others in the world. You will have made the world a better place. You will have elevated your contribution to the collective mind. You will be a happier person. This concept is nothing new, only forgotten.

Life is feeling the essence of Spirit move through the medium of experience. The nature of our being is beyond the physical, the mental and the emotional. Those qualities are simply tools to allow us to learn to experience the magnificence of our spiritual natures.

Feelings are what life is about. Feelings are the angst and joy of the soul as it experiences life in physical form. It's what allows us to bond as humans in time of need, to fall in love, to feel the pain of separation or rejection. Feelings direct our lives, give us intuitions and bring us full circle with an experience so we can move on.

How we respond to what we feel determines how much joy we have in life. In traumatic times it is best to remember the motto "This too shall pass," but not before allowing the intensity of experience to connect completely with you. Feelings that are not allowed the fullness of their experience are certain to change form by showing up as physical condensations of matter that result in pain, sickness or bizarre mental patterns. Feelings are like liquid. Allow them to flow freely and they create interesting patterns, rivulets of diversity that color the landscape of life. Try to contain them and you have a dam of considerable pressure. If the dam is breached, danger and destruction may follow.

"Going with the flow" is about more than passively following life along a trail. It is about flowing with the feelings that will carry you on to new horizons you never even dreamed of. Feelings exist in present time. Feeling is the vehicle that will transport you to being here now. And once there you realize there is nowhere to go. The journey is the destination.

Bothersome emotions are feelings based on past experience and are only occurring now because you are creating an image of an experience that was not felt completely enough to come full circle and move on. They are behind the dam and continue to seek their experience in present time. The river of feeling has a current – some places are rocky rapids and death-defying waterfalls, others are tranquil pools in isolated crooks of the river.

When you immerse yourself in the fullness of feeling, the Spirit is lifted. Spirit quite literally "wells up" inside you. Life is experienced richly in a uniquely human way. Life has a purpose. To assimilate learnings through the medium of experience that assist the soul in its evolution toward higher consciousness while incarnate is the purpose of every soul.

We are created in the image of The One so The One may experience itself as humanity and humanity may experience itself as The One. As diverse manifestations created in the image of The One we each bring a unique perspective to experience. As mirrors of The One we exercise full creative power over the reality we find ourselves in. This is the beauty and the lesson of free will. Free will is the exercise of opinions, judgments, priorities and intentions to consciously or unconsciously form the reality one is surrounded with.

When free will changes its mind before an attracted reality is fully experienced, the result is an existence filled with conflicting intentions. If this happens over and over, many of these intentions go unconscious. Eventually the result is chaos and confusion in a person's life, and an inability to know how they are causing it or even an awareness that they are doing so. Life feels broken or fragmented and the person relinquishes his or her divine creative nature to sources outside the self. The person is left with a feeling of powerlessness and blame, usually seeking salvation from an external source.

The choices you make in every moment either bring you closer to knowing your godliness or separate you further from it. There is an easy way to tell the difference. When you respond to a situation or person, does it feel uplifting or draining? When you go through your day do you feel empowered or powerless? Anything that causes you to feel regret, remorse, a need to prove something or a need for vindication separates you further from knowing your intrinsic divine nature.

My purpose in this book is to teach you how to recognize the ideas you have that cause you to get stuck as you move through life. By unblocking stuck areas you are more capable of attracting what you want with clear and focused intention. For intention to be clear, it must be free of the emotional baggage that overloads consciousness with respect to your goal. You'll find that the farther you go with this, the more general and all-encompassing the qualities of feeling are, affecting nearly every significant outcome in your life.

As you recognize stuck points, you will find yourself discovering deeper and deeper levels of your emotional programming. For instance, what began as the feeling "I feel awful that I didn't get that big client to sign with my company" could, upon deeper examination, lead to a feeling that you never snag the deals that are important because you're not really that good at what you do. Continuing to expand upon that feeling, you notice you have a nagging suspicion that someone else could do the job much better than you. You fear you are not really worthy or qualified to have the success you long for. You feel like you are and have always been a failure, but that you can fake it enough to get by. Exploring that feeling further, you are struck by the cold hard truth that – at least in your mind – you are a failure. What value does a failure have to society or even to one's own self? At the core you feel worthless, with no value or justification in even being alive, because you have nothing to contribute. You are completely vulnerable to further emotional injury, either from self or the world around you. See how that works?

It doesn't have to be that way. A life-line to expanded awareness reveals itself when the judgments surrounding such feelings are released. I will show you how.

Sun sparkling -

Moon reflecting -

Off the mirror of being.

The moon pulls high and low tides of feeling.

The full moon drawing me out,

The new moon pulling me within.

Sun sparkling over the waters of a new day;

I surrender to the flow.

ก. มังตาว

2

Finding the Shortest Path Home

In my early thirties, during an intense spiritual "seeking" phase of my life, I had a recurring dream that varied in content but always had a common theme. I would be trying to go somewhere. The destination could be hundreds of miles by car, a few miles by foot or just moving from one part of a building to another. I always got sidetracked and frustrated because I just couldn't get where I wanted to be. Everything was so complicated and there were so many choices! The shortest route was always the most forbidding and would often occur to me but I would resist, usually because it appeared too frightening or unknown to me, or too dangerous. It always turned out to be the only way I could get where I wanted to go. I would end up using that route eventually anyway, after much delay. It was never as dangerous or frightening as I had imagined. In one dream I was in a car with a confusing and detailed road map. Another time I was on a mountain pass in a blinding snowstorm. In all the dreams I at first tried to skirt the area by going around. Yet the frightening route was always more expedient than I ever would have imagined and not nearly as forbidding and dangerous as I had believed. When I surrendered to the path I must take, I always arrived quickly at my destination, amazed at the simplicity. I always arrived at the conclusion, "That wasn't so bad. How easy! Why did I resist this?"

The dream that really drove the point home for me in vivid detail was a dream where I was at a swimming pool complex and was searching for a way to get from the shower and dressing room upstairs to the pool located down below. I tried all kinds of dead end hallways. I noticed a dark somber old man standing at the top of a steep and narrow, barely lit stair. He pointed with silent finality down the stairwell. It looked dark, dreary and forbidding. It had hard, rough concrete steps that curved out of sight about half way down. For some reason I trusted him. He appeared to be the caretaker of the place. I looked at him with a mixture of hope, fear and uncertainty. I thought, "I've tried everything else so here goes." I took only a couple of steps down the menacing stairwell before I was effortlessly whisked, almost instantly and as if by magic, to the swimming pool below. It was almost as if the intention alone was enough. It was exhilarating and amazing!

I have always interpreted my own dreams based on the emotional "hit" I get. Looking back on this one, the shower and dressing room area represented preparation and cleansing. The dark man represented my inner guidance and an understanding of the "darkest" parts of myself. The dark descending stairwell represented the darkness of my emotions and a fear of "lowering myself" into them. The pool represented the healing waters of spirit. At the time it occurred I didn't understand it. It was years before I realized the frightening but expedient path in all these dreams was the route through the emotional landscape.

During the same period in my life that I had these recurring but varied dreams I was asking the universe for rapid spiritual growth on a regular basis. When all I got were painful emotions and experiences that seemed to recur in various yet similar circumstances, I began to feel disillu- sioned. I wanted the path to enlightenment to be clean and quiet, like a private meditation near a peaceful stream. When I realized my feelings *were* the path of rapid growth I really got scared and depressed. I wondered why my path couldn't allow me to be a teacher, healer, psychic or any- thing more glamorous than simply allowing the experiences of my shadowed heart.

When one surrenders to the flow of feeling, Spirit is invited to ride its currents. Almost everyone is familiar with the feeling of purification that occurs after the release of intense feelings. This is because Spirit is allowed to move. Feelings are the liaison between Spirit and Body.

The difference between feelings and emotions is that what we usually think of as emotional is feeling tainted by judgments held in the mind. The mind orchestrates intentions, structures beliefs and keeps track of judgments. Spirit empowers mind to create the reality you experience according to your intentions, beliefs and judgments. Although this is sometimes a conscious process, it is often something we are not aware of. When we are unaware of how the perceptions of our mind create our experience, it's as if we are living in default to them. This feeling of dis- connection from Spirit causes us to feel as though we are victims responding to circumstance when in fact we are constantly the powerful creators of what we experience. Feelings are pure experience. Emotions are feelings influ- enced by and perceived in a certain way by the mind with a judgment attached. Do you see the difference? Emotions are feelings influenced by the viewpoint of the perceiver. By let- ting go of judgments and allowing the feelings their pure experiential nature, Spirit becomes more present within the body. Spirit has no judgments about experience, it only wishes to experience.

The judgments we make about situations, people, feelings and ourselves prevent the fullness of our experiences by limiting our perceptions. If you examine an emotion you do not want to have, you will invariably discover a judgment that is attached to it. Drop the judgment and be willing to feel what the feeling is all about. You will need a dedicated, quiet space in which to do this, particularly at first. If all you feel is the desire to avoid it, go with that. It will fade away eventually if you stay with it a while. Then explore the feeling you were avoiding. You will find that feeling also dissipates, either gradually or suddenly. If another aspect of the feeling asserts itself, let go of any judgments you may have about it and willingly feel its essence. Try this for yourself.

Each time a judgment is dropped, you create more compassion in the world. First you can learn from the situation because the resistance to experiencing it is removed. The fullness of the experience creates a broadened perspective. A broadened perspective creates greater tolerance. Tolerance inspires you to become interested in others. Interest in others creates compassion in the world.

Emotions un-tethered from the judgments that were attached to them begin to reduce their emanation and transform into something more elevated, more pure, more divine if you will. The emotion transmutes into pure feeling. Its purpose is fulfilled by the experience and it no longer needs to send the same message. For a period of time, clear space opens up in consciousness, a quiet serenity I call the Void. The more time you can spend in the Void, the more peaceful, yet energized your moments away from it will be. In an ancient Chinese practice of breathing and energy work called "Qi Gong" - pronounced "chee-gong" - this Void is referred to as "the emptiness". I've also heard it casually referred to in other circles as "zoning out" or "going to another planet for a while", among other descriptions.

The interesting thing about being in the Void is that it is usually followed by a period of euphoria that invites new experience. It is our human tendency to "fill the void", so to speak, because our purpose on earth is to have an abundantly experiential life. An abundant life is one that is absolutely fascinated and totally involved with whatever one encounters, literally a love of life. It is full presence and awareness in the moment at all times. Some experiences will be more pleasant than others. Allowing feelings and experiences to pass through your life rather than getting stuck by struggling against them is what opens the space for you in which to create something new by changing your intentions and beliefs.

We will always tend to fill the Void with something. The way to attract what you want is by becoming more aware in every moment of judgments and opinions you may have that you may not have been aware are creating your life as you see it now. Awareness of these beliefs is the first key to change. A belief is simply an opinion with enough faith attached to attract the experiences that will bear out its truth. Judgments and opinions, being emotionally charged, emanate powerful creative vibrations. Notice how you are judging what you are feeling. Then let the judgments go and surrender to the feeling. You will be absolutely amazed at how quickly things can change when you do this one thing and make it a habit.

If experiences present themselves to you and you avoid them because you judge them to be unacceptable, you will only create them more tenaciously in your life. You will expend so much precious attention trying to control the feelings you don't want that you are not free or able to enjoy what is right in front of you now. These suppressed feelings are the voices you hear in your head like old tapes that nag at you during your waking hours and complicate your dreams and sleep at night. Allowing yourself to experience feelings as they arise will keep you returning to the Void for rejuvenation followed by euphoria and the manifestation of new experience. Returning to the Void is to the Spirit what sleep is to the physical Body. Sometimes they overlap a bit.

We are on this earth to feel alive and to learn through experience. Feeling is the evolutionary catalyst for our spiritual nature. Feelings that are allowed their full experience eventually lead back to love and compassion. That many feelings are painful to experience is part of the lesson in the school of life. We must each come to know ourselves through the medium of our personal reality in order to effectively raise the consciousness of the planet.

After integrating an experience we can move on to another. An experience is helpful spiritually when its full feeling is allowed and judgment is withheld. Some experiences must be repeated many times, perhaps over many lifetimes, before the resistance to them becomes worn down. Sometimes they inflate to such an "in your face" intensity they can no longer be avoided and are finally reckoned with. The key is to stop judging them. Judgments prevent the fullness of experience. Nothing new can be learned from a situation when an edict has been passed that limits the freshness of perception in the present moment.

Through lifetimes of incarnation on earth in a physical body, a being integrates its experiences as lessons, eventually remembering its oneness with all of creation. To recover this memory while incarnate is the intention of Spirit and the catalyst to a broader, more divine level of awareness that ripples forth into the collective mind. As individualized aspects of The One we evolve at our own pace to greater levels of empowerment. As a collective we are also evolving. The hate and terrorism that exist in the world reflect disowned fragments of the collective mind. It may take lifetimes for a soul to discover the limitations of certain patterns of thinking and belief, but each experience created by those beliefs is a step forward. All paths lead home, to The One.

The challenge to go within and explore the unwanted feelings that lie there is not a license to take them out on the world. It is an opportunity to know yourself deeply, truly and thoroughly in a way you may never have considered. It is an internal experience. Expressing emotions outwardly is fine as long as you are not using others as targets for your blame, anger or intimidation. But you must always feel whatever is there - begin to notice the judgments that are associated with the feeling. You must become quiet to do this. It's a kind of quiet that, while it appears uneventful to an outside observer, may feel like an implosion. You are allowing feelings to bubble to the surface of your awareness that may have been brewing below the surface for most of your life.

Yes, you may be furious that your husband cheated on you, your mother was an alcoholic and your father sexually molested you when you were seven. But instead of blaming them for ruining your life, notice the judgments you made about yourself, others and about life that have affected who you are today and how you are living your life. The list could go on and on but here are just a few possibilities: "Men are jerks," "It's not my fault," "I'm ashamed," "I'm not loveable," "I can't help myself," "I don't deserve happiness," "Mother didn't love me enough," "Sex is bad," "I'm bad," etcetera, etcetera, etcetera.

If you insist on holding on to these judgments all you will take away from your experiences is a feeling of powerlessness. Feeling powerless leads to resentment and anger. If you remove all the judgments surrounding these experiences, what are you left with? Pure feeling. Feelings of pain, abandonment, neediness, powerlessness and most of all vulnerability. Feelings of worthlessness. Feelings most of us hope and wish we will never have to experience again. Feelings we hope to deny by creating judgments that obscure their presence in our lives.

The interesting thing is, if these feelings are allowed space within your being rather than suffering the congestion that holding judgments brings, they will find their way out very quickly. Holding on to the judgments locks the feelings firmly in space and time: the space is in your physical and emotional body and time is the event you cannot let go of that perpetuates your discomfort.

Others are interested in your emotional pain only to the extent that they have either healed their own pain or that they need a diversion from it. Those who have accomplished a great deal of inner healing are interested in others because they are not distracted by their own problems and truly want to help. Emotional pain is the great equalizer and experiencing it without judgment fosters compassion for the pain of others. Those who need a diversion from their own pain are interested in others as a kind of "me too" camaraderie or as a way to feel better about themselves by comparison or by taking attention off their own pain. They want to know that someone else is as miserable as they are, or possibly more so. It doesn't make sense, but this is how many people find comfort in their emotional pain. It's a classic example of the old adage "misery loves company". Since they don't believe they can do anything about it they need to know others are just as miserable. It somehow validates that they are not "worth less" than the next person.

Feelings of worthlessness and vulnerability are at the core of most human emotional need. If you dig deep enough you will discover judgments designed to protect you from feeling vulnerable. Feeling vulnerable is an expression of the pain caused by the separation of self from Spirit that is part of the human experience. Our souls seek a way back home, to The One. That is the evolution of Spirit. To remember and feel your divinity while incarnate is the pinnacle of human experience.

Your life is your own experience. It is personal to you and no one else can do it for you. No one else perceives things in just the same way and no one else's expression of self is exactly like yours. The challenge is to discover what is there, to see, recognize and feel experiences from the inside out.

You are completely unique. There has never been anyone quite like you before and there will not be again. Isn't that amazing? Your feelings and experiences are more complex than the most advanced computer, and infinitely more mystical. There is so much to learn about yourself if you are willing to feel the truth that lies within. There is no pain, shame or embarrassment you can feel that has not hurt, shamed or embarrassed more people than you can possibly know. If you allow yourself this humility you can move on to something new and much more exhilarating.

We are deep sea divers
Swimming through what is all around us;
It is also within us.
It is so close to us that we cannot feel it,
And yet we cannot be separated from it.

3

The Convergence of Science and Spirit

The worlds of science and spirit are converging. We've all begun to notice it. More and more the laws of physics, once considered the hardest of all the sciences in terms of cause and effect theory, are becoming less law and more theoretical. Spiritual disciplines, once considered esoteric and mythological by many, are being embraced in a much more general way by larger and larger portions of the world's population, including physicists. Thoughts affect results. It was a major revelation when physicists began first discovering that the presence of an observer affected the outcome of an experiment.

Modern physics has now begun to embrace this phenomenon. That the thoughts of an observer can and do influence the outcome of an experiment is an idea mystical spiritual traditions have embraced since recorded history. It is a recognition that we are accountable, to a much greater degree than has been previously thought possible by mainstream thinking, for the direction and quality of our lives. It is now a question of "What are the possibilities?" We don't really know what the limits are or even if there are any. It may be more a question of how expanded we can allow our consciousness to become, both individually and collectively.

The intrigue of magic or for things considered miraculous is the result of a memory lingering in the background of awareness. The fascination with things that appear magical is a yearning to return to our fully aware and empowered state, our divine nature.

Children love to listen to fairy tales because their soul memory of magical realms and infinite possibility is still quite fresh, untainted by the social conditioning of what is considered possible. The relatively new Harry Potter tales are loved not only because the stories are highly entertaining and well written, but because Harry accepts his magical powers easily and uses them with good intention. Often criticized by certain teachers or classmates who resent his natural abilities and humble fearlessness, his goal is only to heal his inner pain by discovering the truth about the mystery that has shaped his life. That goal should ring a few bells - it's what we all want. His tolerance and desire to restore fairness and justice endear him to those who will open their hearts to the goodness of his intentions, and their minds to the possibility of alternative existences.

The draw to the miraculous is a yearning to return to the ways of Spirit, to feel the force that moves the universe and wields its power in wondrous and creative ways. People often have religious conversions after observing or experiencing something miraculous because it jogs their memory into remembering Spirit. There is a recognition of Spirit, acting in mysterious ways that invite heart, mind and body to participate. When something magical or miraculous reaches the physical realm, Spirit has managed to find a gap in the layers of resistance created by judgments and limited thinking.

Sometimes we return to the miraculous during sleep. In dreams we experience many things that are magical or fantastic, but during the dreams our mind accepts them as perfectly natural. Dreams have always had significance in connection to Spirit because they connect emotions in the subconscious to the guidance of super-conscious spiritual realms. Dream messages often appear obtuse, so much so that they are often disregarded.

Magic is here at all times waiting to be remembered. All we have to do is become fully present in the moment, right here, right now. There will never be any more happiness than there is now. Happiness in the past or future does not exist except as a yearning to bring happiness to the present. When there is nowhere else you would rather be, you have involved yourself in the power of the present. There may be caverns in your mind and corners of your heart that occasionally rumble with dissatisfaction. Be grateful to them for revealing the fullness of the human experience and Spirit will miraculously transform your life. The alchemy of Spirit is a burning up of your dark aspects that humbles your heart and opens your mind. It is a magical brew of temptation, challenge and transformation.

We are here on earth to experience the amazement of living on it. We do this by balancing the four aspects of life we are given to experience it with: emotional, spiritual, physical and mental. It means living purely in the moment and savoring all it has to give you. Any form of judgment by the mind about the experience is a resistance to what is. The mind can choose to let go and have the experience, observing in quiet fascination or it can cause imbalance by making judgments that do not allow the fullness of the experience. By not experiencing fully, the being becomes "polarized", continually attracting similar types of unwanted experiences like a magnetic pole.

If this sounds simplistic it is because we tend to make life much more complicated than it needs to be. You don't need incense, ceremony or ritual unless you just enjoy it and feel good using it. You don't require the blessing of a minister, priest or rabbi although you may choose to have it. You don't require anything outside yourself. The Spirit of The One is already within you. It is the universal force that creates, destroys and permeates everything. You need only open yourself to the experience that is surrounding you at this and every moment. No one else can do that for you. It is the cross you must bear, your own cross, created by the imbalance of many judgments and much resistance. It is not glamorous to take up the cross of your disowned emotional fragments but it is exceedingly simple. The results are miraculous. The wisdom gained is profound.

The skill of learning to live according to the fresh input of each moment is training for life. It is meditation in action. It is the source of power. It is the frontier of the miraculous.

Each one of our perceptions and experiences is directly affected by the qualities of the intentions generated by our conscious and subconscious minds. These qualities are affected by judgments about feelings generated in response to conscious experience. Intentions are tempered by these qualities emanating as a result of experience. This is why it is so difficult for most people to change patterns in their life they want to change. Their intention is one thing, but the quality of the signal coming from their subconscious is laden with emotional mandates. These mandates are stored in the subconscious mind and steer the ultimate direction life will take, not always in the direction a person might consciously wish to go.

The subconscious mind is the great storehouse of life's experiences. It is also the seat of your emotions. Because the prime directive of the subconscious mind is one of protection and survival, anything you have experienced that had emotional consequence for you is more charged with creative power, or the lack of it. Let's say, for example, that when you were a small child that you either, out of ignorance or curiosity, did something your parents considered wrong. You didn't really understand it much but a while later when you asked for something you wanted you were told, "You don't deserve that." Or maybe you were punished immediately and told you deserved it. You didn't really understand what went wrong, but the subconscious mind, fulfilling its purpose of protecting you from pain, indexed this event in its limitless storehouse for use in automatically evaluating all future circumstances that may have a similar flavor. The effect may have been to limit your curiosity about learning new things, or to be fearful of venturing into unknown areas where you might be able to learn something you are now ignorant about. Unfortunately, this kind of ignorance breeds even more ignorance and escalating feelings of undeserved-ness.

This is the way emotional patterns become firmly embedded in our lives. Like attracts like. What you think about and what you feel, whether intended or unconsciously, draws it to your life. People sometimes say opposites attract. Opposites only attract in order to more firmly define their separateness from each other. In doing so, they more clearly define for themselves and the world what they identify themselves as being. But the idea of self as separate is a grand illusion, created by Spirit to allow the vast multitude of experience that is possible while in a physical body. Recognizing self as an aspect of the overall divine order is the challenge of Spirit. In the twenty-first century, more and more are hearing the call to come home. Home to Spirit.

The more awareness you bring to a particular situation at any moment, the more consciously you can create.

Awareness is enhanced by feeling whatever is there. Awareness is nearly synonymous with feeling, because to be aware of something implies there is something to be aware of. Being human, our method of becoming aware is mainly by feeling. Even visual information is processed very selectively, mostly by the way we *feel* about it. We are kinesthetic, experiential beings. By being present and aware, you not only shape your reality, you begin to notice how you are doing it. It's a mystical cause and effect phenomenon - every time you change your viewpoint – cause – you experience a different manifestation of reality – effect.

We all do only the best we can at any given time. If life hands you a bowl of lemons you can make lemonade. You can even sell lemonade and turn your trouble into industry. Or you can decide it's too sour and go thirsty. The point is, we always encounter the unexpected. We don't usually know what is going to be next for us to experience. Our thoughts and perceptions create our reality at every moment, but so much of our mind operates at a subconscious or unconscious level, not to mention super-conscious (spiritual), that we often don't consciously know what we are going to create next.

One of the things that makes life so tricky is how much of what we experience is in charge of the subconscious mind. It has been said for the last generation or so that we use only ten percent of our brains. The idea is that we only *consciously* use ten percent. The other ninety percent is performing all the autonomic functions of our bodies that we don't have to think about, as well as being in charge of our habits and imaginations. At the time this idea was introduced, it was revolutionary. But lately the perception of that ratio has changed. Now the accepted theory is that more like ninety-six to ninety-eight percent of the functioning of our minds is done on a subconscious or unconscious level.

[I would guess that in future years that ratio may encompass an even broader gap, to the point where we realize the part of consciousness that we are aware of is fractions of a percent, maybe even hundredths of a percent, or smaller.

We are just beginning to realize the ocean of awareness that makes up the mind in addition to the conscious part we are aware of. If we include the super-conscious mind, or spiritual aspect, it is undoubtedly true that the conscious mind functions in miniscule fractions of a percent in relation to the whole, perhaps extending to a nearly infinite number of zeros before the integer "1" is added. Yet even this kind of definition would place limits on something that is really not quantifiable or definable.

Have you ever paid attention to how thoughts and images, verbal messages, songs, memories and dreams of the future seem to randomly drift in and out of your awareness without you really trying to put them there? That's your subconscious at work, ruminating through the files of your experience, both tangible and intangible, including sights, sounds, smells, tastes, feelings and ideas. The more cluttered your thinking, the more information your subconscious mind is trying to manage, with much of it spilling out at random moments into conscious awareness. The more this occurs, the less focus a person has in accomplishing the things that are desired in life.

That's not to say that daydreaming is of no value. When the mind wrestles with a problem or creative challenge, daydreaming is often the quickest and most enjoyable path to a solution or breakthrough idea. Some people may have a habit of taking long walks to accomplish this. For myself, I've had some of my most inspired moments taking long drives by myself.

This kind of activity, because it is somewhat hypnotic
in nature, demands less of the conscious mind and gives the
subconscious a chance to ruminate and process information
and ideas uninterrupted, occasionally spewing a useful idea
into the realm of conscious awareness. And since driving a
car is a learned, habitual behavior controlled by the subconscious mind, the act of doing it for a long period of time
gives the conscious mind a rest.

The neat trick of subconscious control is that because
the prime directive of the subconscious mind is one of
survival, you are able to do this quite safely. I'm sure you've
had the experience of driving from Point A to Point B and
remembering little or nothing of the drive in between?
Most people have experienced this road hypnosis, at least
for short periods of time. It sometimes makes people
nervous because they believe they must always be in conscious control. But because the subconscious is the ultimate
multi-tasker and is motivated by survival and protection, it
is able to accomplish the feat of taking you safely to your
destination while your conscious mind floats from one idea
to another. The main benefit of learned habitual behavior is
the ability to do things effectively without having to
consciously be aware of every aspect of doing it.

This important task of your subconscious mind – to
file away all your learned behaviors so you don't have to do
them slowly and deliberately – makes life much easier.
Once the subconscious mind takes over you do them habitually. We simply couldn't be productive at all if we had to
think through every single act before we did it. A great deal
of childhood learning is acquiring these habitual behaviors,
such as how to tie a shoe, ride a bike or brush your teeth.
How you drive a car or play a musical instrument is much
more efficient with the aid of habits learned by the subconscious mind.

To reiterate, the most important motivator of the subconscious processes is to protect and preserve the being
while it is incarnate. The subconscious is not logical or dis-
criminating and takes information that is given to it quite
literally. One of the reasons it creates habits is to make life
easier so the conscious mind can focus on what's important.
Unfortunately, some of these habits may be detrimental,
particularly habits of behavior that are based on judgments
of past experiences. A judgment made about a painful
experience while it was occurring may cause the subconscious mind to "protect" you by not allowing you to feel it
fully or remember it well later. In your emotional pain it
sensed danger and reacted the only way it knew how, by
shutting down the feeling. This may have been the most
appropriate thing to do at the time.

However, as life goes on the trapped feeling continues
to try to re-assert itself, or stays hidden but causing a vague
discomfort with life. As long as the conscious mind main-
tains its judgments about whatever the subconscious is
holding to protect you, any attempt to release the feeling
will be unsuccessful. The subconscious has become habitu-
ated to keeping it out of your conscious awareness. Because
the feeling is still there but not allowed to move, it festers
and rumbles below the surface of awareness, creating
dissatisfaction, anger, sadness and pain that seem to have
no reason or relationship to the present.

If you will consciously release the judgments long
enough to allow the fullness of the feeling, just observing it
with curiosity while allowing it to swell within you, you
grant it passage to move out. As the feeling moves, Spirit is
drawn in, refreshing and revitalizing you. The tasks of the
subconscious mind become fewer, as it no longer has to
place attention on hiding or controlling the feelings it has
now released. This frees up your attention on all levels to

attract and create new, preferably more enjoyable experiences. Your thinking is now clearer and less cluttered by unwanted thought patterns. You may more effectively attract circumstances that please you by the way you think. Pass the bowl of lemons, please.

In opening up to the creative flow of ideas,
More come to me,
As if they are being guided home.
Creativity waits in the random chaos of the unmanifest,
Emerging when a gateway is opened.

4

The Continuum of Knowing

As you become more adept at recognizing and releasing judgments you will discover deeper and more profound levels of them. Being able to let go develops a skill in self-observation. By simply observing with interest you allow the voice of intuition that comes from a place of compassion, reminding you of your connection to The One. It is a shift from reacting (emotionally judgmental) to observing (Spirit). This shift creates a two-way conduit from heart to Spirit that allows a being to both feel and observe experience simultaneously or to move seamlessly from one way of knowing to the other.

I will describe a continuum of knowing that ranges from intuition to feeling, emotion and mind. They are intertwined. Intuition is a hunch, a feeling about something that cannot be explained but is immediately recognized by the person having it as right or true. It is non-verbal knowing. Intuition appears random and chaotic. Intuitions are thoughts generated by the super-conscious aspect of mind. Because they present themselves in a non-sequential way that is both subtle and with the appearance of being random, they are often disregarded by the conscious rational aspect of mind as irrelevant.

Feelings are the realm of experience. They are nonverbal integrations of the experiential. Pure feeling knows only its existence in present time. Pure feeling is a conduit for intuition. Like intuition, feelings arise spontaneously in the present moment. Feelings are the knowing of experience in a direct way.

Emotions are feelings clouded by judgments arising from the conscious mind that limit their experience. Emotions know only the need for release. Their origination in pure feeling is not static – it is the judgments created by the mind about the feelings that cause them to become stuck. Emotions that are allowed to flow without judgment eventually return to pure feeling. Emotions that stay stuck limit creative ability by absorbing all of your attention.

The conscious aspect of mind is the organizer. It is threatened by the chaotic nature of intuition and pure feeling. It knows, through the evaluation of past experience and societal conditioning, which it uses to form beliefs and judgments designed to create a more orderly experience of life. In its attempt to maintain order and control it forms judgments that limit a person's ability to be intuitively, fully present. What it can't figure out it will rationalize. What it is not prepared to deal with it will store in the vast recesses of the subconscious.

The conscious mind tries to understand absolutely everything. Mind's biggest problem with feelings is that they are disorderly, irrational and often unpredictable. Trying to talk about them and understand them does not have the same effect as allowing the feelings as they are.

Paradoxically, when you drop the judgments that transform a feeling into an emotion and allow the feelings their pure existence, you shift into an intuitive mode that makes sense of them in its own way. The realizations may seem irrational. You may discover relationships to past experience that lead to profound insights, and these insights may make sense to no one but you. This is whole brain understanding, not necessarily analytical.

A highly evolved mind re-learns its creative ability through a pure decision and intention to do so. Such a mind has been trained to hear the silent voice of intuition by releasing its judgments. The flow of un-judged emotion transmuted back into feeling invites intuition.

At this point the person has come full circle and consciousness is expanding, spiraling outward. Interestingly, drawings of spirals are found in the cave paintings of nearly every primitive culture studied. Although their exact meaning has never been completely agreed upon by archaeologists and historians, I regard them as universal symbols for an expanding consciousness that is one with an expanding universe.

Intuition is unreliable for most people because it receives so much interference from the chatter of the mind. Intuitive hunches don't always make sense to the mind. This is exactly why the mind must be still in order to receive them. Any thought that arises in reaction to an intuition tends to misguide its perception. It's like trying to tune into a distant AM radio station with chatter, buzzing, hissing and screeching sounds obscuring the signal. Intuition is a feeling that knows without knowing how it knows. It is wisdom emanating from the heart and soul. It seeks the trust of our minds, but mind does not want to trust that which it cannot figure out.

Profound personal insights can be realized intuitively when emotions are allowed to be felt by removing the veil of judgment that emanates from the mind. When we feel bad about ourselves it is impossible to separate the judgment from our experience. The pain of criticism inflicted upon ourselves limits our ability to be fully present in the moment. It causes us to feel separate from the strength and power of our Spirits, a most painful experience. It is the classic "fall from grace" described in the Biblical book of Genesis as the beginning of the human experience. In order to stop judging yourself and re-connect to Spirit you must first fully experience the pain of being separated from it. It is the path of least resistance, the path that flows swiftly home to The One.

By experimenting with these principles, mind can learn to allow intuition. The more you recognize and drop judgments the better your life will become. Once mind recognizes this it will be more willing to welcome the signals intuition offers and intuition will become stronger and more reliable.

Heart feels what truth is.
Soul knows what truth is.
Mind creates what truth is.
Body experiences what truth is.

5

The Four Aspects of Experience

There are four aspects of being that co-exist while we are alive in a body: mind, heart, body and Spirit. They are designed to work together. Each aspect offers a resource for experiencing wholeness. One should not dominate at the expense of the contributions of the others.

In a dualistic way of thinking (positive versus negative, good versus evil, light versus dark, male versus female, etc.) the projective aspects, mind and Spirit, are more male in nature. The receptive aspects, body and heart, are more female in nature. However, all four aspects do contain both projective and receptive qualities.

Mind thinks. Spirit knows. Together they intend a projection that creates the realities we each experience – our personal universes. Because mind works mainly on a subconscious level, many of the realities we find ourselves in do not appear to be manifestations of our intentions. The intentions of Spirit are super-conscious – beyond conscious awareness – so they too do not always appear to be manifestations of our intentions. Spirit inspires and observes from a neutral perspective, a detached awareness. The conscious part of the mind has the task of ordering life based on conclusions it draws about experience.

Body, being receptive, experiences this personal universe *unconditionally*, and tends to store emotional charges that are not released. It is the recipient of experience, whether that experience is embraced or avoided by the mind. It feels experience in a physical way that includes both its direct sensory perceptions through the five senses as well as the containment of emotion. Physical pain and illness often result when blocked emotion is held in the body. Love your body for holding the emotions you are not ready to look at. Love your feelings and your body will be healthier.

Heart is the receptive aspect of being that feels its way through experience. Heart is constantly in touch with Spirit through the conduit of feeling. When your heart is not clouded by judgments of the mind you will remember how to listen to it. You will be in present time with your experiences and will know intuitively how to use your mind to create what you want next. Heart has no ulterior motive. It seeks only to feel the guidance of Spirit and to relay the feeling of its experience back to Spirit.

The mind does not like dealing with messy feelings or being limited by the heaviness and constraint of a body. If mind had its way, we could think ourselves to enlightenment. We would also be able to physically fly or easily astral project our spiritual essence at will, unencumbered. But while in the world the heart, soul, body and mind must integrate harmoniously in order for Spirit to achieve its purpose for being in a body. In fact this was one of the two basic commandments Jesus of Nazareth gave his followers:

"Love the lord your God with all your heart, soul, strength and mind."

When these four aspects have lost their sense of connection to The One, the mind judges and projects its fantasies about reality, transforming feelings of the heart into stored emotions of the body and mind. Emotions are created at the juncture where feelings are judged by the mind. The mind then responds to these projections rather than allowing the feelings to bring up whatever is there. As a result body and heart feel disconnected from Spirit. The being lives in a sea of resisted emotion or becomes physically or mentally ill unless emotional healing takes place.

In an ideal state, heart senses both body and Spirit by feeling, and mind responds to the intuitive inner guidance. For example, a person who has been declared terminally ill may recover completely and go on to live a healthy life for years. Sometimes illness can trigger an emotional reckoning that heals the heart. Heart then re-connects with Spirit and physical healing occurs. This has happened to many people. The fact that it doesn't always happen is neither a reason to dismiss the possibility nor a justification to judge someone who does not heal this way. Our journeys are personal.

For most of us emotions rule our lives by our resistance to the underlying feeling. Mind is not capable of containing them, at least not for long. Body cannot contain them without becoming overwhelmed and sick or in pain. Spirit waits patiently for emotions to transmute into the purity of experience. They do when the mind stops judging. When that happens, the body is re-vitalized and the heart rediscovers its intuitive connection to the guidance of Spirit. One aspect no longer dominates. There is a return to balance.

Feelings are human. From triumph to tragedy, we can't help feeling something. We can block a feeling, but blocking it only transforms it into something annoying and unhealthy. Blocking a feeling often creates numbness or apathy, which is only an illusion that no feeling is present.

If you feel an underlying deep sadness in your life, dropping to the bottom of your grief doesn't mean you'll never come up again. But refusing to experience it will insure that it won't go away. It will just keep hanging in there like a black cloud in your life. Others will feel it and pull away. That may cause you to feel even more down. Let yourself be in your grief completely and unashamedly, as a small child would. Don't worry about where it will end. Just grieve. Be in the moment with it. Notice what judgments you are making about yourself when you feel your worst. These are the keys to your liberation. How does it feel to be the way you are judging yourself to be? Keep going until you've checked it all out. At some point the feelings will be transmuted or lessen.

If you feel grief without a reason you can identify, it is important to allow yourself space to experience it. You may come to a realization about past experiences that are shaping your present view of the world. In the rush of discomfort during an unpleasant experience, perhaps a judgment was formed that created an unconscious belief you now live by. It's been stored safely away in your subconscious, filtering perceptions so you attract experiences that bear out its truth.

If no major realization surfaces, experiencing your grief will still be helpful on some level. The fleeting nature of feelings does not allow them to stay static once they are unlocked from the prison of judgment. So let them flow.

Sometimes our emotions are so repressed they have impacted upon themselves. We release and release and still there seems to be no end. We must peel away layers of the onion, so to speak, and access the hot, fiery core that is contained within it. Remember, this too will pass.

Emotions are like cries for help from the soul. They are the navigators that steer our course in ways that feel out of control to us. If we don't like the course we are on, we must become more conscious of the judgments we hold that are attracting our experiences.

If we could feel purely, without judgment, we would know what to do at all times. Feelings are the conduit for intuition, which works best when the mind is in a passive state. But most of us have pushed our feelings away because of judgments of the mind, transforming them into emotional baggage. They have become a nuisance. They are under the pressure of containment and burst out at inappropriate times because our bodies and minds can no longer bear to hold them.

The non-acceptance of feeling runs parallel to the non-acceptance of intuitive, subjective realities that dominates much of the collective mind perspective. The prevalent idea is that feelings, intuitions and mentally fabricated experiences are not rational, therefore they are not real. Saying "It's all in your head" is a common way of dismissing emotions. In a way it's true. Emotions are feelings of the heart judged by the mind. They become stuck by the judgments of the mind, or head.

Emotions don't go away when they are suppressed, but they are transformed when allowed their full experience without the judgments. This can be an internal process. It doesn't have to be done by "venting" or "letting off steam". Don't try to do it by bringing someone else down to your level. Feel the depths of whatever it is - within yourself - and let it go. Remember that thoughts are intentions to the universe. You only need to feel what is there. You are not trying even the score with any real or imagined opponent.

I don't even recommend that you externalize your emotions unless you can do it in a controlled environment that does not put anyone at risk, including you. You will not gain anything by taking your bad feelings out on someone else and if all you do is complain, others will tire of hearing it. If you can set up an environment that allows you to externalize your feelings safely without harming others, then go ahead and do it. If anyone else is present they need to know what you are doing. Don't leave them bewildered and wondering "What the hell happened to you?" That said, sometimes controlled externalization is a powerful tool to get in touch with deeply buried feelings. I describe an example of this in the chapter titled *Negative Emotions*.

Here are some ways to begin evoking the flow of feeling again in your life. Notice whatever comes up for you when you do them. Most of these use the physical body as a starting point. Physical processes are often very effective ways to draw out the slow poison of stagnant emotion.

Dance – You can be spontaneous or take a class. Be sure you choose music that makes your body want to respond. Free yourself and play with it. If you feel embarrassed, explore the embarrassment while you are dancing. Do it alone, then do it with a group and notice any differences you feel. Allow yourself to be uninhibited and *feel* the music. You don't have to be good.

Martial arts and Yoga – Tai Chi, Karate, Kung Fu, Jujitsu, Qi Gong and Yoga are powerful ways to channel inner strength and personal power. Martial arts drills can also be a way to release stress or pent-up anger.

Therapeutic full body massage and deep-tissue bodywork - In an earlier time in my life I made a living for several years as a professional massage therapist. It's amazing how much emotion lies stored in muscles and connective tissues in our bodies. In the business we called this phenomenon "muscle memory". Sometimes the emotion connected with a traumatic event can be released in a single session. The cumulative effect of regular massages over time helps release and integrate many emotions. This often occurs at unexpected times, not necessarily during a session.

Passionate lovemaking – Sometimes freeing up sexual energy provides a surprising emotional catharsis. Occasionally I have experienced feelings so primal and overwhelming in the moments *after* an orgasm that it felt as if the foundation of my soul was trembling with both the ecstasy of relief and the angst of being human. On more than one occasion I sobbed intensely. I didn't always know where the feelings came from but it was amazing to observe them without judging them. It felt indescribable to just let them be what they were and watch them fade away.

Sports – Choose a sport that appeals to you and participate if possible. Even spectator sports draw out emotions. Watch people during a football game and notice how much you can tell about a person by their reactions. Notice how you judge them too. Then notice it in yourself.

Movies – Watch a dramatic movie that is emotionally powerful for you. When an intense scene presents itself, follow the emotion to its source within you. Notice what you discover there. Wallow in the quagmire of feelings. Allow yourself to explore it without shame or judgment. Don't try to stop the feeling until it has run its course. It may very well put you in touch with unresolved feelings connected to an event or with repressed emotions you have about yourself. Don't try to stop the feeling and don't try to hold on to it either. Just feel it until it has run itself out.

Here is an example of how watching a movie worked for me in letting go of past grief. I once watched the movie *Black Beauty* for no particular reason but was stunned by the outpouring of emotion I felt at the end of the movie, even though it had a relatively happy ending. I sobbed as if heartbroken for nearly fifteen minutes. The movie was about a wonderful horse that had lived a variety of experiences at the hands of many masters, some kind, some not kind. In the end, he was returned to the pasture of his youth, set free.

The movie brought back strong feelings of connectedness and a sense of loss about a horse I rode for many years as a pre-teen. Ajax was an extremely spirited, but well-trained horse that intimidated inexperienced riders. Years after I left home, my father sold him. The horse lived in his new home where he enjoyed a couple of young riders for several years. Then he was re-sold to someone who, I'm told, later sold him to a company that collected horses to process for dog food. His last owner considered him unruly and did not appreciate the magnificent creature he was and thus, poor Ajax was not able to spend his old age retired in a pasture like Black Beauty.

I had learned of his fate many years after he had been sold for the last time. It came up in a casual conversation about horses when I was visiting my parents. I had been devastated. I tried not to show it because I could see my parents were sorry they had mentioned it when they realized how it upset me. When I watched the movie *Black Beauty* a few year later, all the feelings I had buried came rushing out to be released. Over fifteen years later I watched the movie again and was surprised how it did not affect me the same way. I had moved through the grieving the first time I saw it.

Sometimes the most unspectacular moments
Are the most profound.
You must take time to open your eyes;
If you are only worried about survival
You will miss them.

6

Begin Where You Are Now

Your current expression of life is the sum total of all your experiences, realizations and beliefs in the form of judgments. Yet each moment is only as genuine as the presence you bring to it. The less clouded by prejudiced perceptions of the past, the more fresh and voluptuous the present moment. The more you let go of a past filled with conditioning that does not serve you today, the more infinite are the possibilities that can transform your future.

Each day is an opportunity to wipe the slate clean, invoking a creative vacuum within which new realities can be fashioned. The past affects you only to the extent that you continue to live within it. Welcome each day with gratitude as a new opportunity to live each precious moment to its fullest, as if it is the only moment you have. Truthfully, now *is* the only moment that ever exists.

Memory is only useful as a tool for learning to creatively enhance your life now. Re-living the past serves no purpose and keeps you stuck in the unhappiness of knowing you either are not now experiencing the pleasurable moments you are re-living or that you cannot let go of unpleasantness that occurred in the past. Both pull you out of the present. Fond memories can be very seductive, but dwelling on them does not allow you to be present with what is happening now.

When painful memories keep re-asserting themselves you must take charge of the situation. Instead of waiting for the memory to re-assert itself another time, actively seek it out. Go where you do not want to be - on purpose. Allow yourself to feel the memory in a way you have not yet done: by exploring all its aspects and allowing every feeling it stirs to bubble to the surface of your awareness. You will likely notice many judgments about the situation or your feelings regarding it. There is a feeling you did not want to have. Because you avoided it, you did not experience it fully at the time. This is why it keeps re-occurring in your life, either as a similar manifestation in the world you experience, or as a bad memory you cannot let go of. The way to heal is to truly feel it: on purpose, willingly and without judgment.

Many of us avoid feeling by distracting ourselves. This is the essence of compulsive busy-ness. Some people stay so busy they never have time to feel. The busy-ness becomes an addiction, like escape through alcohol, food or drugs. Like excessive busy-ness, these substances are used to escape from feelings.

The workaholic is a person who does not wish to feel something. It's okay to love your work. You may love your work so much that your whole life is devoted to it. However, if it becomes a substitute for feeling, it is an addiction to escape. For example, a psychologist may help patients heal emotional trauma but not feel comfortable with her own friends, family or inner self. A church minister may tend to his flock seven days a week and be adored by his congregation but have difficulty resolving personal relationship issues. A productive businessperson may be so immersed in her work that when she is not absolutely swamped, she doesn't know how to take time for herself or enjoy a leisurely vacation. Work often becomes a well-disguised addiction to avoid some kind of feeling.

Surrendering to the *feeling* of what is happening *now* is the path to grace. Only by feeling whatever it is you are resisting can you begin to let go of it. "Be here now" became a popular idea after Baba Ram Dass (Dr. Richard Alpert) published a book by the same title in the early 1970's. It was a time when the seeds of spiritual evolution had found fertile ground and begun to sprout in greater numbers.

In order to be here now we must learn to feel the present moment. In your daily activities, whenever you think of it, stop and ask yourself, "Where am I? "Who am I being?" When you have an idea of that, ask yourself, without judging where you are or who you are being, "What does this feel like?" Then take a moment to really feel it. Make this a habit. This is the path of power. This is where feeling discovers intention. Intention is what created where you are now and what will allow you to create a new reality if you so choose. By ceasing to resist what is, you are empowered to intend a new vision.

Shackling your creative ability by funneling its power into resistance only creates limitation, frustration and a feeling of powerlessness. Until you have embraced your anger, your hate, your fear and your grief, including everything negative that frightens or upsets you now, you cannot know freedom. You must see firsthand what they have to show you about yourself. Until you do you will continue to be burdened by the baggage of your emotions.

The fact that a person makes the same mistakes over and over does not mean that person is not learning. I've noticed many are searching for ways to speed up their soul evolution. The collective mind is waking up. My purpose in writing this book is to trigger insights for others by sharing my own experience of truth in a way that may inspire realizations.

We search for something to tie it all together. We wish to feel more present in the moment. We wish to feel at peace in our hearts. Feelings are the link. Feelings are to Spirit as blood is to the body. They are the life force that carries experience to every level of the soul. Feelings flood a being with the intensity of life. Their flow nourishes and cleanses Spirit as blood does the body.

By feeling the present moment we allow the purity of experience that invites Spirit to transform our lives. This is grace. This is the space of non-judgment that forgives all, accepts all and knows all. In the sweet surrender of judgment lies greater awareness. This is the grace of the present moment.

Impossible as it may sound to you at this point, inner peace starts by beginning to feel whatever you are feeling right now. What is it that you feel right now? What do you feel most of the time? Have you fallen into habits of feeling that have no real connection to present time? Perhaps you feel anger, resentment or a deep sadness much of the time. It gnaws at you because you do not really face it. You do not know where it comes from and you are not sure you really want to know. You fear falling into a bottomless pit of emotion in which there will be no love and from which there will be no escape. This fear is the absence of love. You are afraid that if you give audience to your feelings they will consume you. You cannot love what you are afraid of, but you can be certain that what you fear is in control of your life.

You go on living, feeling some rumblings in your emotional body but not really listening to their messages. Eventually you may become so numb to their presence you no longer realize they are there. Catatonic complacency replaces a zest for life with all its myriad experiences. Eventually you feel there is something missing. You may be successful on a surface level and have accomplished all your goals and still, something is missing. You vaguely remember a time in your life when you expected more, and you felt more.

Begin right where you are now to start experiencing whatever it is you are feeling. If you have too many judgments about doing this, or about the emotions you feel, this will prevent the fullness of your experience. It will stop you from being able to let go and move on. You must first begin to notice the judgments surrounding your perceptions in order to understand how they are placing limits on your ability to fully embrace life.

Begin to recognize many of your current thought processes for what they are: judgments that place limitations on what is acceptable to experience. Begin to notice where or how these judgments originated in your thought processes. Are they useful to you today? Were they ever useful?

When we make a judgment about something in our lives – another person, an experience or even ourselves (which, by the way, occurs almost continually) – we place limits on our ability to perceive in a pure way. We have already decided what our perceptions mean to us and the freshness of the moment is lost. Continuing to make judgments about people does not allow your perception of them to change, even though the person may have changed. Similarly, if a person has not changed much and your perception of that person changes to embrace a different judgment than you had in the past, you will find your experience of that person to be suddenly different.

This also applies to "positive" and "negative" experiences. So-called "negative" experiences most often contain the greatest potential for soul growth, because they drive the experiencer to look deeply within. Such experiences are challenges to expand your ability to experience compassion, humility and oneness with others. When they are resisted the lessons are overlooked, and one continues to repeat similar experiences. Often they are acted out over and over with the same people. Habitual behaviors become so deeply and co-dependently entrenched that it becomes very difficult for a different pattern to emerge, even when both parties would like to change.

It is important to step back a bit and start noticing what judgments are being assumed as incontrovertible truths. Remove the importance from the need to be right in your assumptions. You must become vulnerable in this way for new possibilities to reveal themselves. Our vulnerable moments are the most potent with learning potential. This is why young children learn so quickly. They are not afraid to be vulnerable. Vulnerability breaks down the walls of judgments and allows the purity of experience. It invites deep realizations within the soul.

Sometimes it is more convenient to make judgments. We think it will save time. We think we don't have to deal with the feeling of an experience if we have already determined its hierarchy of importance or meaning to us. We tell ourselves we have too much going on to deal with that. We make a judgment to keep things simple so we don't have to think about them. Unfortunately, the judgment becomes attached to the feeling that was not allowed experience. This results in an emotion that reappears automatically whenever it is triggered.

Many times people make judgments about those around them, blaming others for the circumstances they find themselves in. Recognize that every judgment you make about people and experiences are reflections of yourself. There is no person or experience you encounter that does not have something to teach you. There is no judgment you can make that does not reflect back yourself, revealing your weaknesses to others and diminishing your sense of self-esteem. All gossip, all judgment passed on another, is rooted in a misguided desire to feel better about oneself. In not recognizing our unity as the collective expression of The One that we are, we hope to raise our stature by lowering that of someone else. It is always self-defeating. The only way to raise our stature is by dropping *all* the judgments about people and experience and allowing the differences. If you can see yourself in everyone you meet and appreciate an expression of yourself in each person, then you have truly raised your stature. You will have helped yourself and at the same time, made the world a better place. We are not separate. We are one. The next time you meet someone you feel like judging, realize that he or she is holding up a mirror for you. If you don't like what you see, you still have healing to do.

So how to stop judging others? Awareness of judgments as they occur is the first step. It all comes back to yourself. As long as you continue to resist feeling whatever is inside, you are making judgments about yourself. Not wanting to recognize these self-criticisms or the feelings that accompany them, you project them onto people in the world around you, who unknowingly live them out for you. You reciprocate by mirroring different projections back to them, knowingly or unknowingly, that they perceive in you. Like an old magic trick, "It's all done with mirrors."

Judgments that arise in daily life inhibit your willing-ness to experience, preventing the integration that could otherwise occur when you allow the fullness of your feelings. Experience is a feeling thing, after all. It is tactile, sentient, present and powerful. To learn through your expe-riences, you must first feel them fully. Without feeling there can be no integration, no journey toward spiritual whole-ness. If all you have been feeling for years is your resistance to something, you must first feel the depth and scope of your resistance. Only then can you move on to feeling what-ever it is you were resisting. Not doing this will continue to attract the same experience or something similar over and over. Why take third grade over and over if you can get the lessons the first time?

Begin by feeling whatever it is you are feeling right now. Continue doing this for the rest of your life.

"Would you tell me, please, which way I ought to go from here?"

"That depends a good deal on where you want to get to," said the Cat.

"I don't much care where—," said Alice.

Then it doesn't matter which way you go," said the Cat.

"—so long as I get somewhere," Alice added as an explanation.

"Oh, you're sure to do that," said the Cat, "if you only walk long enough."

—from *Alice's Adventures in Wonderland*
by Lewis Carroll

7

A Brief Synopsis of My Spiritual Journey

My philosophy cannot be encompassed by any particular doctrine I am familiar with, although it contains elements of many. My views have evolved greatly over the years, as dynamic and changing as life itself. I strongly believe that spiritual experience is internal and spiritual wisdom comes from within. For me organized religions do not bring me closer to a personal experience of divine communion. I've always been an independent sort.

By the age of ten I was frustrating my school teacher by refusing to accept limited thinking when it came to the idea of life on other planets. "Why can't other life forms exist that don't need the same things we need on Earth?" I remember asking. Part of me already understood the idea of parallel universes or alternate frequencies of being-ness that could exist in what we consider inhospitable environments. My disposition was always to question limiting ideas.

By my twenties I was questioning everything about my Protestant Christian background and began exploring the relationships between it and philosophies of the Far East as well as earth-based pagan religions, Native American teachings and all forms of mystical teaching. Interestingly, when I stepped back to get the big picture I found more unity among them than diversity. The only thing separating them is dogma. The inner experience of Oneness, of transcendental communion with God, Nirvana, spiritual ecstasy, salvation from sin, whatever you prefer to call it, was the common thread among them all. It is the indescribable that so many have tried to describe, the personal connection with one's own divinity that cannot be preached from a pulpit but only experienced within one's own heart. The fact that there are so many religions expressing this in a myriad of ways speaks volumes about the diversity of perceptions on planet Earth.

I began to consider myself a "spiritual seeker" at about the age of twenty-three when I began studying the work of Edgar Cayce, a famous clairvoyant in the early 1900's. I was seeking to expand my understanding of the role of the life of Jesus of Nazareth within the collective consciousness. Raised as a Christian but feeling the traditional view was not the bigger picture, I began a quest. Cayce had strong ties to Christianity, which I needed for my comfort level in the beginning. Cayce's work expanded my view of the life of Jesus tremendously. His trance readings discussed such things as reincarnation and the law of karma. This led to a study of eastern mysticism and yoga. Later I explored Native American teachings, New Age materials, energy healing and martial arts.

All these interests supported my growing conclusion that we are spiritual beings of divine origin and of the same source. It seemed obvious to me that all major religions point to the same ultimate truths, albeit with different formats. It is the difference in our personal choices, our early conditioning and our unique perceptions that cause fundamental truth to be interpreted and defended so many different ways.

In 1980, at the age of twenty-six, I read Aldous Huxley's book published in the 1950's called *The Doors of Perception*. Huxley had participated in a controlled psychological experiment with the use of mescaline and described his experience of it. His vivid descriptions of the experience intrigued and inspired me. His lucid chronicle of the power and presence of everything he could perceive resonated with truth and clarity. In the preface to that book Huxley quoted the poet William Blake who once wrote, "If the doors of perception were cleansed, everything would appear to man as it is, infinite." I was curious to explore this possibility and wanted to experience more of the infinite. Although I had already experimented with and been amazed by psychedelic mushrooms, mescaline and peyote, I decided to try hallucinogenic substances with the idea of expanding spiritually.

Hallucinogenics have been used by indigenous cultures for accessing spiritual realms and inducing visions for as long as humanity has known about them. Usually they were reserved for certain members of a group, the shamans. Eastern mysticism teaches that opening someone to higher levels of awareness without proper preparation can cause paranoid or psychotic types of reactions. From my experience it seems that preparedness simply refers to the person's spiritual readiness to embrace a larger perspective.

"Hallucinogenic" is actually a misnomer for vision-inducing drugs (referring to substances such as LSD, mescaline, peyote, psilocybin mushrooms). It implies that what is seen is not real when it actually is as real as any other reality. The mind shuts off somewhat from its normal filtering of information to allow the experience of a broader awareness, what I call inter-dimensional thinking. Psycho-active substance is a more accurate term. The substance activates the psyche to take in a bigger picture and integrate a much broader perspective.

The things I read and heard about LSD convinced me of its superior ability to induce inter-dimensional thinking. I had previously stayed away from it while dabbling in other mind-altering substances because of the negative information about it that pervaded mainstream thinking.

The first time I "dropped acid" (LSD), a new door definitely opened. It was as if the windows through which I saw the world - "the doors of perception" - had been cleaned and I was seeing clearly for the first time. There was nothing more important or more fascinating than what was right in front of me. Objects had a textural detail and rich-ness that vibrated with a rhythmic pulsation hypnotic in its feeling of universal-ness. It defied explanation. My neural pathways felt electric. When I played my favorite music the vibrations surged through my body as if I and the music were one. I felt a resonance with everything I perceived, as if I was not separate from anything. I felt euphoric and at times outside my body, as if observing myself from a dis-tance. Sometimes I felt my consciousness in two places at once. The world was a source of complete amazement and absolute profundity. I had insights and understandings that felt extremely spiritual. In fact it felt as though there was nothing that was not spiritual. Everything was alive and creation was a swirling potpourri of magical manifesta-tions. Everything I perceived appeared to have its own dimension of existence, yet merged effortlessly into the whole. I remember thinking, "This is not hallucination. This is how we are supposed to see!" The matters of day to day living seemed insignificant, even comical. I would never be the same again. The depth of insights I realized and the broadened level of awareness were simply too profound to disregard and forget.

Although I continued to experiment this way for a period of time, I soon realized I had taken what I could from the experience and must learn to create that state of wonder and cosmic oneness on my own, without the drug. I gave it up for good and then the real journey began. There were my emotions, messy as ever. I began to realize, although I did not want to admit it, that the biggest hindrance to my spiritual fulfillment was the emotional baggage I carried with me. I wanted to "be here now" but did not know how! And although my excursions with psychoactive substances had revealed wondrous things, it is not a path I would recommend. Aside from the physical toll it places on the body, it is an escape from the lessons the emotions would have you learn about your day to day life and identity if you would simply stop judging. I knew intuitively that it is possible to reach the same levels of euphoric vision and power without resorting to the use of chemicals.

My era of personal growth workshops began. I had tried transcending the emotions by an act of will but found they always came back with a vengeance. Eastern philosophers had talked about the need to transcend the emotions. Apparently I just didn't know how to do it. I tried quieting the mind through meditation but my inner critic would either chatter incessantly or fall asleep. I got the message my mind was giving me: "I don't want to play!"

A key discovery in every personal growth workshop I did was that allowing the experience of resisted emotion allows a bit more of the inner Spirit to bubble to the surface. It fans the flames of Spirit fire, causing it to shine more brightly. It works for two reasons: (1) we are experiential beings and (2) allowing the flow of feelings bypasses the mind. The recurring dream I used to have about the shortest path to where I wanted to go being the dark, scary, forbidding one was trying to point me in the right direction. It is the path of experiencing feelings without judgment. Feelings can be dark and scary and our minds forbid us by judging them. But it is the path of least resistance. It is the path that will eventually quiet the mind. It is the path that will elevate consciousness to a higher state of awareness and a profound sense of kinship with all other souls. It is the path with heart.

If thoughts are things
Then things are also thoughts;
Attention charged with feeling
Attracts condensations of matter
That precipitate form.
Old habits die hard.
Doubt collapses reality,
Belief calls it forth.
Faith tests belief in the unmanifest,
Feeling draws it into being.
If you will change your mind,
You will surely transform your world.

8

What Do You Think?

Y ou are what you think. You are also what you
think you are not. Does this seem a little
bizarre? My point in bringing this up is that
whenever you resist someone or something by thinking you
are not that, you invite the essence of its presence into your
experience. It doesn't matter whether you actually want to
experience it. The simple quality of having an emotional
charge on the idea of experiencing it is what gives the experience its gravitational pull toward your reality.

Certainly for many, that idea brings up fear. Follow
this line of thinking for a moment: "Well, my thoughts run
amuck constantly with random ideas I have no control over.
I can't control my thoughts so I can't control my life. I'm just
a victim of my thoughts. God must have put them there, so
God is in control. I'll just give it all up to him and forget it.
It would be so much easier not to have to deal with all this
stuff myself. My nature is just too sinful. Human nature is
just too sinful. We are inherently bad and easily tempted to
do the wrong thing. The only hope is for someone or something to do it for me, because I'm unworthy and worthless,

I'll never be good enough. Let me just beg forgiveness for even being alive and some spiritual leader will tell me what to do. Someone with a direct line to God. There, that feels better. I don't have to think about it now. I don't want to think about it either. It's just so much easier knowing that whatever happens is God's choice for me and I'll be at peace knowing that nothing that happens to me is my fault. All I have to do is what the spiritual leaders tell me to do and no matter what a pain the circumstances in my life are, I know that when I die I will be rewarded with everlasting peace and happiness for tolerating this lowly existence here on earth."

See how that works? Does any of this thinking sound familiar? Most of us have had one or two of these thoughts run through our minds at some point. Just mentioning the possibility of thoughts directing one's reality can cause a mind to race with lightning speed down a trail that leads to its disempowerment. Many would like to experience something different than what they are now experiencing, but few are willing to take complete responsibility for the way things are now in order to change it.

[It's a bit like the repetitive dream pattern I described in the chapter *Finding the Shortest Path Home*. In those dreams I was always looking for an easier way than by taking the dark, forbidding path that ultimately turned out to be the fastest and most painless route to my destination. At a core level, the destination we all seek is to return to our spiritual nature – communion with God, if you will. The most direct path is through the quagmire of emotional debris we accumulate as we go through life, perhaps thousands of lifetimes in a multitude of differentiated identities.

The study of hypnosis has revealed that during the time when the conscious mind is relaxed we are more open to suggestion, memories flow easily and the imagination, the language of the subconscious mind, is more active. Setting aside a quiet time to relax the mind and focus on goals should be a priority for the effective achievement of those goals. This is the power of creative visualization, most effective when done in a relaxed state. It places attention on desired outcomes while you are more empowered to attract them than in your normal every day waking awareness.

There is an obvious difference between the workings of the conscious and subconscious minds but it is not always easy to say where one ends and the other begins. They operate as a continuum in our mental space. The conscious, subconscious and super-conscious parts of the mind orchestrate and control the realities we each experience.

When we break up emotional patterns by releasing judgments and allowing the feelings they controlled, the situations they were attracting are no longer pulled into our lives. The subconscious mind has less work to do and the conscious mind is less distracted. The body is more relaxed. And the Spirit is pleased, because it's main reason for being in a body – to feel its aliveness - is once again at the forefront of experience.

The reason thoughts become out of control is because we give up control of our lives to an outside source. Thoughts are attracted to the emotional carnage of past hurts that were resisted and never fully integrated. The more these thoughts build up in the subconscious mind – the seat of the emotional body – the more fragmented and confused we become. Our goals become scattered and diffuse until we eventually don't even know what we want. We find ourselves unable to effectively create any kind of life that is truly meaningful to our core selves. This is because we don't really know our core selves anymore. Usually sometime after the age of about three or four, we lost touch with what we really and truly - deep inside - want to express in our lives.

How to get it back? The first step is to begin to recognize all the areas in which you are making judgments about self and others in your life. These are your cues that something is not right. Start by picking a judgment you have about someone you know and isolate it. Recognize it for what it is – an attempt to make you feel better about yourself. Then imagine what it would be like to be someone who had the quality, belief or behavior you are judging and allow yourself to explore it. If you are honest with yourself you will discover that part of you already supports or exemplifies this quality, belief or behavior. You may not do it in the quite the same way, or perhaps it's a pattern you once exemplified that you have stopped doing, a behavior you have now disowned. It could even be that a part of you would like to be able to be whatever you are judging, but due to the judgment attached, you simply won't allow yourself!

Judging others is a sign that all is not well on the home front - your inner bliss is compromised. Recognition of the fact that you are judging others is the beginning of spiritual healing. Because once you get inside and start looking around, you begin to realize that all those judgments are really self-judgments in disguise. You were projecting all of your self-judgments on others to avoid confronting the insecurity and vulnerability you feel when you try to live life according to the inner wisdom of your own heart. Judgments obscure your life mission and render you powerless. They make excuses for not being able to create the kind of life you dream about. Give them up!

Another way to regain control of your life is to recognize that whenever you are resisting some idea, part of you is already buying into it. That part may be a faint ribbon of a thought you either don't acknowledge or don't remember, but it's enough to cause you to take a stand against it.

Whenever there is a need to assert your position, there is a seed of doubt.

I realize I am leaving myself wide open here. I've written an entire book devoted to my personal view of emotions as they relate to spirituality. I do believe there is a difference between presenting insights and beliefs for others to examine and share in as they see fit, and forcefully pushing ideas on others by manipulating their fear. Both methods offer hope, but preying on people's fear offers a powerless hope that is unhealthy to the evolution of the soul. With apologies to the evangelists, the need to convert others to your way of thinking is a demonstration of doubt. A true spiritual leader always leads by example. If someone is converted by such a person, it is because the converted senses the truth emanating from the heart and soul of the person who converted them. The words that come out of that person's mouth are not what convince converts of their truth. It is the presence of the spiritual leader, the confident knowing that radiate from his inner being. It is a presence that is *felt* by the people who are attracted.

Some evangelists are quite successful because in addition to telling others their personal truth, they exude charisma and an acceptance of others that attracts people to them. By withholding judgment and meeting people where they are they create a feeling of safety for their followers.

Yet others command their religious fervor like dictators, asserting that they were called by God to strike fear into the hearts of the lowly and save them from their sinful natures as they themselves have been saved. Unfortunately many of their converts, in their zeal to spread the word, become spiritual bullies. They intimidate others with their self-righteous indignation and pious holier-than-thou attitudes. This kind of behavior is not helpful to anyone, least of all themselves.

I've read and heard the teaching of evangelists that say we must know a "healthy fear of God". That whole phrase is an oxymoron. These same people also say that God is love. Yet fear cannot exist in the presence of love. Fear is the absence of love. I'm not talking about instinctual fear, which is necessary for physical survival. I'm talking about judgment-driven, mind-shriveling fear that incapacitates your ability to connect with your inner self and create the life you would like to live.

Instinctual fear is part of our biological programming – it's hard-wired in so that in the event of an emergency we react in a way that preserves the physical body. It's the only form of healthy fear that exists. Even though it's healthy from a self-preservation standpoint, the excess of adrenalin released during a fearful event can be quite challenging for the body to deal with, occasionally triggering things like heart attacks or strokes. Yet this instinctual fear has a spiritual purpose: to preserve the body long enough for the person to recognize his inner nature, learn from it and re-connect with the divine spark. Fear that is emotionally driven – that is to say, by feelings with judgments attached to them – is *never* healthy, either from a physical, mental or spiritual perspective.

My insights about evangelism have emerged as a result of experiences with some who are closest to me – painfully close. I have four siblings and we are all very spiritual and/or religious people. One heard her calling during mid-life, although she had always been religious. In her mid-forties, she embarked to seminary school and for the past fifteen years or so has been a very successful Methodist minister, well-loved in the various congregations to which she has been assigned. She and I have very different views about spirituality but she comes from a place of love, kindness and forgiveness that I respect. I suspect she got to that place by being faced with the challenge of living with a husband she loves who did not always – and perhaps still doesn't – share all of her beliefs. I admire her resolve to follow her heart.

Another sister converted to Catholicism when she married her high-school sweetheart. It may have been a matter of convenience at the time, but she also found herself attracted to the ritual and decorum of it that wasn't part of our Protestant upbringing. And she remains today a very kind and loving Catholic with a terrific family of children and grandchildren. I honor her for that.

My other two siblings, a brother and a sister, were converted and "reborn" into Fundamentalist Christianity about twenty years ago at separate times and in separate areas of the country. I respect their decisions to follow their truth but find it a constant challenge when communicating with them to keep my thoughts to myself while listening to them carry on about how *they* believe. Nothing they believe is subject to scrutiny or refute, and anyone who attempts to do so is immediately chastised with verbal lashings of self-righteous condemnation.

I love them both and when we avoid the subject of religion or spirituality we get along fine. Yet because this is an area that is obviously important to all of us, there is quite a gap in the breadth of things we are able to enjoy together. I hear their views but find it is more productive toward maintaining a relationship with them to keep my own to myself. It feels a bit like what I would describe as spiritual tyranny. It is certainly a challenge I have wrestled with. While writing this book, I have contemplated the possibility of backlash from the Fundamentalists, simply because my family experience has caused me to be very aware of it. I know the forces I am dealing with. But I also know that writing it is important to fulfill the life mission I have set for myself.

On the other hand, I am grateful to my Fundamentalist siblings for causing me to look within and examine myself even more than I otherwise might have. At one point not long after my brother's conversion, I decided to give his way a thinking a fair shot. I attended a church service with him and his wife. He seemed to have found something that worked for him. I, on the other hand, was still out and about, examining everything from Gnosticism to Buddhism to Native American Lakota teachings.

I was told that at the end of the service the preacher would call those who were inspired to come forward and receive the Holy Spirit of God to transform their lives – to receive the "gifts of the Spirit". My brother had done this at a revival and had shocked himself when he fell on his knees and began speaking in tongues. I was definitely intrigued and had to see what this was about. Before I went to the church, I prayed fervently that I would be shown, or know within myself, once and for all the true meaning of the teachings of Jesus Christ. "Let me understand the true message Jesus came to give," I begged. I was ready, if I felt the call, to come forward at the appropriate time.

Yet the time came and went. When others stepped forward, I stayed in my seat. I knew then that this was not, and would never be, my path. I believed in the truth emanating from the life of Jesus, and still do, but this way was not mine. What a relief to really know that! Today, I prefer not to use any definition at all to describe my spiritual views. How can one define something that by its essence is indefinable?

I've questioned beliefs, both my own and those of others, to an exasperating degree for as long as I can remember. And the belief I always return to is that truth is personal. Our thoughts, judgments and opinions create our experience of life on earth by miraculously attracting to ourselves circumstances that reiterate the thoughts, judgments and opinions we hold dear, either by choice or default. And unfortunately for those who continue to resist their current experiences, the attracting power of emotion emanating from the resistance of them will continue to generate the experiences!

Once you have recognized a judgment, if you can release it long enough to feel the underlying feeling it was "protecting" you from, you will discover a level of awareness of your core self you may never have accessed before. It can leave you feeling quite raw and vulnerable for a while. If you continue to withhold judgment as you burrow through these deeper levels, you will eventually reach a quiet space within yourself, what I call The Void. When you return your awareness to the world of matter again, the feeling is often euphoric. With each release of blocked feeling, the subconscious mind has one less bit of experiential data to store and filter experiences through in its job of keeping your life on track.

So yes, by writing this book and espousing the idea that resisting something means part of you is already buying into it, I'm laying myself wide open here for scrutiny. Yet I hope most people who read it will not see it as resistance to what is, but rather an opening to possibility. I'm encouraging you to push the envelope of your awareness by letting go of judgment and discovering what lies beneath. Every time you expand your awareness in this way, you move a little closer to the divine source within you. Resistance to what is keeps you in hell. Experiencing what is shows you the way out.

Give me something to believe in -
On this I strongly feel.
It gives my life direction;
My faith's a steering wheel
To guide me to experiences
That I consciously create.
Through all life's simple choices
I guide and own my fate.
And what I know for certain
That is absolutely true,
Is that my truth may really
Not be true at all for you.

9

Your Experience Demonstrates Your Truth

Truth is the essence of all that is. The essence of experience is truth. Anyone who incarnates in this earth plane is a vessel for truth. Most simply don't know it. Our lives are a manifestation of our deepest beliefs. Through the omnipotent power to create, our minds and Spirits intend and believe our realities into existence, manifesting our personal truths. They generate experiences that bear out the truth of our beliefs. Many beliefs are so unconscious we act through them automatically, attracting our life experiences unknowingly. When we consciously choose to believe and have faith in our beliefs, miracles happen.

When a person intends to create something, the more emotion or feeling that is attached to the intention, the more surely the manifestation will occur. Unfortunately, fear and self-doubt contain emotions that create unwanted realities for many. If the fear of or resistance to experiencing something is greater than the confident expectation of a desired result, the fear or resistance actually brings the undesired outcome into existence. If this outcome has been in place for a while, the resistance toward it will perpetuate its place in your life.

The purpose of experience is for truth to evolve within the consciousness of the person experiencing. Truth includes subconscious beliefs you may have as a result of conditioning by society or judgments made based on previous experiences. Personal truth is not necessarily the same for one person as for another, because we are individualized aspects of The One.

As you sojourn through lifetimes, personal truth varies from one incarnation to the next, but each experience of your truth brings you either directly or indirectly closer to home, closer to The One. We live our truth while participating in the realm of being human. It is an art and a craft, one you can hone to greater skill in this lifetime by becoming more aware of your judgments, beliefs, underlying intentions and feelings. Whether or not we like what is happening in our lives is largely determined by how consciously we are aware and in control of the many layers of our personal truths.

Every experience is an expression of your personal truth. Even your so-called personal failures, lapses of integrity, etc. are created by the beliefs you hold present most consistently. Increasing your awareness of your personal truth will allow you to fashion life in a way that is most meaningful to you. Intense experiences, however challenging, offer much opportunity for integration of the Spirit with body, mind and emotions. Every failure has within it the opportunity to learn something to assist the soul in its evolution.

Failures that repeat themselves reveal a resistance to learning the lesson that could be taught from experience. The challenge of resistance is to ask yourself, "What do I not want to feel?" Willingly feel into whatever that is. Great relief lies there. That is where the gold is. The fullness of each experience is the gem that needs to be mined. When resisted experience is embraced, it dissipates like sand through a sieve. Then the Spirit can move on to something new. Until it is, the person will continue to experience similar situations or the same situation repeatedly. Feeling the resisted experience will often reveal insights and realization.

Resisted emotions must be fully experienced in order to let them go. If this is not done, they continue to drain the joy out of the present moment, because part of your self is still living in the past. You are not recognizing that what was true then is not necessarily true now. It only appears to be true because the resisted emotion continues to attract experiences that bear it out. The repetition of unwanted but similar experiences reinforces the belief that continues to be a magnet for them. If the resisted emotion is allowed to run its course, the belief and its resulting experience have room to move. They can change. To experience your spiritual nature in a human body, you must first learn how to feel. Drop the judgments and immerse yourself in the fullness of feeling.

If you are afraid to go to the bottom of your emotions, if it looks like a bottomless pit of despair that you'll never see the end of, it's because you've never had the courage to look at it. There is, at some point, a bottom. You may even bounce off the bottom a few times before you begin to come back up, but the bottom is there.

Enlightenment would have no value if we didn't know the pain and fear of living in darkness. The power of enlightenment is that we also know the darkest depths of despair. We appreciate what we have learned from despair. A person becomes stuck in despair when they continue to make judgments while attempting to explore what they are feeling. This is the trap many fall into.

Many of us fear what would become of the world if all were willing and able to embrace their personal power in creating their destiny. This is exactly why Jesus of Nazareth was crucified. His teaching was threatening to those who controlled society. He encouraged his followers to embrace their own godliness and personal power. At the same time he taught humility, non-judgment and seeing yourself in others. He understood the power of intention and utilized it to perform miracles. His personal power drew much attention to himself but he advised his listeners, "These and greater things shall you do." His compassionate acceptance of the lowest in society was inconceivable to those who did not wish to lose status and who could not see themselves in those they despised. His views were considered dangerous.

I know many feel they could never live up to the example he set and that it is blasphemous to even consider the possibility. Such people believe his incarnation was unique. It was unique because it was his own expression of Spirit, but at all times he insisted that all are children of God and have similar powers. He chose to empower others, indicating his highly advanced spiritual nature. For example, when others were healed by his touch he told them, "Your faith has made you well." He did not claim to be a healer. He said the healing lies within the person being healed.

Truth is very personal and the manner in which a person experiences life is a demonstration of that truth. Truth accommodates the interests, prejudices and lifestyle of the believer. It reflects individual natures, which are dynamic and often change. What is true for a person today may not be true in two weeks or ten years. As truths are experienced through the passage of many belief systems (and most likely many lifetimes), one eventually arrives at a final truth. Belief shapes reality. There is no separation between self and the Universe. It is all connected. We are all one being. We all affect each other by our individual choices and beliefs.

Clinging to a particular belief when it has been demonstrated to cause suffering or unhappiness keeps a person from growing spiritually during an earth incarnation. Discovering these problematic beliefs can be tricky, because we don't always realize we are making a choice. "That's the way I was brought up" can become a very limiting filter in our ability to perceive alternate possibilities. Emotionally traumatic early childhood experiences may cause us to unconsciously choose limiting beliefs that affect our ability to transform the present moment.

Usually a person living in a physical body will only experience inner peace in a moment of serendipitous passivity. The mind accidentally turns off for a moment while attention becomes fastened on some miraculous observation that previously went unnoticed. Sense of self becomes obscure and merges with a limitless sense of beingness. Separation between the inner and outer self blurs and is replaced with a sense of oneness with all of creation. It is a moment of epiphany that, once recognized, ceases to exist. Recognition of something creates it as separate from the recognizer and the being again becomes aware of its separation from The One. The being falls back into the dimension of time as the desire to hold onto that moment emerges. That moment, however, is impossible to re-create. Instead it must be created anew, in the presence of being here now.

There is a way to become closer to this kind of inner peace on a daily basis. By letting go of our judgments about everything, we are able to experience anything more fully. When we experience fully we come into the present moment.

To do this, we must become more completely aware of how many judgments we actually have. There are not only the judgments about other people in our lives. Situations are judged as good or bad to experience. Beliefs are also judged to be good or bad. Most debilitating of all is self-judgment, which is reflected in our attitudes to things external to us.

The more judgments you have about your experiences, the world around you and the people in it, the more judgments you are carrying about yourself and the less you will be able to enjoy life. There is no surrender to the present moment when judgment is present. The fullness of the experience is missed. People say they are trying to live more in the present. You cannot try. You must become totally and completely fascinated with the experience of each passing moment, without judgment. Notice whatever you feel and feel it. You don't have to express it to someone. Just notice whatever is there. Allow yourself to explore the feeling or experience until it passes. If it doesn't seem to dissipate, either you are still holding on to a judgment or there is more there to experience.

Try this on some feeling you consider unpleasant that you would normally avoid. Become fascinated with the intensity of it, the depth and color, so to speak. How does it feel when you are not judging it, but only experiencing it? Amazing, right? Not necessarily pleasant, but powerfully present. The fear is that you will get stuck in it. Let me tell you a secret. You will not get stuck in it, at least not permanently. You are stuck in it when you keep resisting it, because then you cannot let it go. The nature of life is change, but when you are resisting, you are not experiencing and nothing will change as long as you keep resisting. You will just keep resisting the same experience over and over.

When you give up your judgments in order to experience fully, life flows like a river, changing course as the terrain requires. Situations that challenge us are like rapids in the river, causing turbulence and blocking the flow. Stagnant areas gather moss and debris. The urge of the river, like Spirit, is to keep moving. By the same token, our higher selves urge us to keep moving, experiencing the changing flow of each passing moment, allowing The One to become manifest in the physical. Experience is an incarnation of The One. It is The One in discovery of an aspect of itself. Experience is the Spirit in motion.

Vision, intention, action,
Belief and attention
Activate the law of attraction.
Out of nothing comes forth,
By an effortless power,
Manifestation untainted
By the lack of self-worth.
And for those who do not know,
Ignorance decrees
It shall not be so.

10

The Need to Be Right Can Stop You from Getting What You Want

People often drift away from the recognition of the spiritual nature they were born with and won't make an attempt to re-connect with their spiritual roots until pushed by some catastrophic event or traumatic loss. After the age of about three or four, our minds have become accustomed to filtering our perceptions of the world and our experiences in a certain way, based on feelings we experienced in the first few years of being alive. This filtering allows us to be more efficient at processing the constant deluge of information we are confronted with each day, but also limits our perception of what is possible or of what is actually there. Our view of the world settles into a more or less complacent efficiency.

Much of what determines our filtering are judgments that have been passed along to us by those who were important to our survival at a young age. This usually comes mainly from parents but it can also come from any important figure in the child's life. Children at this young age are extremely vulnerable to the limiting beliefs, value judgments and reprimands of those they hold in high regard: those who take care of them. Some of what they learn is obviously helpful and some of it is not. At this point in a child's life, any experience that has a strong feeling attached becomes a permanent part of the filter that processes future information and experience.

The subconscious aspect of the mental body, which serves as an emotional warehouse for stored feelings in addition to carrying out its primary purpose of protection, is wide-open at such a young age and is eager to take on any information it perceives may be of benefit. The information may or may not actually be beneficial. The mind doesn't yet have enough information to feel internal conflict. Information given by those the child respects as important to its survival is given the highest priority.

Later on, when new information is presented that conflicts with this high-priority programming, it is filtered out and rejected. This filtering reinforces the truth and importance of the initial information in the mind of the person rejecting the new information. This is the evolution of the viewpoint of an individual. It is how prejudices are formed. It is the basis of the need to be right.

If the mind perceives that its truth may be threatened by the acceptance of some new information, it will simply dismiss it out of hand. It is important to remember that it is only doing its job. Based on its need to insure the protection and survival of the individual, the subconscious aspect of the mental body at all times believes that whatever it perceives as truth is for the good of the individual.

This truth is the result of childhood programming and sometimes, past-life programming. Since we are all ulti- mately one collective being, whether or not you believe in reincarnation or past-life regression is not really important. As a collective mind, we all have access to the feelings of all experience in all dimensions of space and time. Some people have experienced major healings after being guided through past-life regression while in a relaxed state. Whether or not the events they recalled actually occurred is not as relevant as the fact that recalling them effected a physical, emotional or spiritual healing. The mind was opened to the possibility of a solution and one was brought forward by the subconscious mind. It's yet another example of how powerful our thoughts are in attracting circumstances to our lives.

Affirmations and declarations (I use the terms interchangeably) have become quite popular, almost mainstream. The information stored in our subconscious minds is the great setback with using them to try to create a life experience. Much of the information stored there has an emotional charge that the subconscious uses to filter the conscious mind's perception of what is possible. Declarations and affirmations do work to a limited degree because more focus is placed on the desired outcome than would normally be the case. And the world of matter manifests according to the attractive nature of attention. Yet most people fail miserably when relying only on affirmations to change their lives.

The problem is that the subconscious talks back. These mental thought patterns assert themselves every time you affirm something you really want but have been unable to achieve. If you set a new standard for yourself by reaching beyond your previous limits, the emotional décor that lines the hallways of your mind begins to come out of the woodwork as well. Limiting ideas like "I can't do that", "I'm not smart enough", "I'm not educated enough", I don't have the right experience", "It's too hard", "I don't have enough time", "It will never work", "My parents always said…(fill in the blank)", and the masterpiece of them all, "I don't deserve it!" Often the conflict is so great that after a period of time the person gives up in frustration.

These are just a tiny fraction of the kinds of thoughts stored in our subconscious minds, anchored by the judgments that hold them hostage based on early experience. Because of the emotional charge attached to them, the subconscious has a strong need to be right. But this need to be right, if you hold onto it, will continue to prevent you from getting what you consciously want.

The way to make affirmations and declarations more effective is to notice the feelings and judgments that pop up when you begin to claim what you really want. You must allow them their space – they'll take it whether you want to give it to them or not. They are part of your mental and emotional framework and they have a need to be right. Allow them their space by feeling into them.

Stick with one response to begin with and move on to the others later. When you feel into this long enough you will get to a good basic premise, such as "I'm not worthy" or "I'll be abandoned". Feel it in all of its magnificent limitation. This may leave you feeling a bit raw but as you work your way through it you will find the feeling dissipating. Allow it to fade away. In its place will be the clear space of a quieter mind.

If you continue this process you will reach a point where the possibility of attaining the goal of your affirmation feels more real. The subconscious no longer attaches the same importance to storing a resistance to it.

There is a difference between the transformational power of emotional catharsis and the pure feeling of experience. In recent years people have become more willing to experience their emotions in a cathartic way. Many now advocate it as a path to well-being and psychological wellness. Yet unless the attached judgments are dropped, the healing will not be complete.

Lately, the trend has been to try to bypass the emotions by techniques ranging from simple declarations to the movement of subtle energy systems of the body. These methods have value, yet none of them alone can do a complete and thorough job of transforming unwanted outcomes and emotional patterns.

The element that must be present is the acknowledgment and release of value judgments that are attached to the feelings. Anyone who has received successful spiritual healing or energy healing has done so because they were willing to surrender their judgments long enough for change to occur. For emotional catharsis to be an effective healer in the long run, the person must remove the judgments from the feelings being experienced.

Feelings are the nature of aliveness. We all have them. When there is blame, shame guilt or criticism attached to a feeling it becomes an emotion and has staying power. I've heard some say emotion is literally "energy in motion" and by some definitions it is. Since I define emotion as feeling with judgment attached it is no longer energy in motion. So often the energy gets stuck in value judgments that transform the purity of feeling into the poison of emotion. Emotions that involve pious self-righteousness or a sense of superiority are just as toxic as the ones that diminish a sense of self.

At a small personal growth training I did many years ago, we did a useful exercise that demonstrated how our judgments interfere with our ability to have good relationships, keeping others at a distance. We worked in pairs, with a facilitator to assist us. One person sat passively while the partner was prompted to make observations about him (or her). It went something like this: The facilitator would say, "Notice something about his face." The person in the hot seat would take note of something and acknowledge but not say what it was out loud. Then the facilitator would ask, "Does that make you feel superior, inferior or equal to this person?" The answer was given and the facilitator would move on to another question such as, "Notice something about how this person carries himself." After acknowledgment the question was again presented, "Does that make you feel superior, inferior or equal to this person?" Other points followed, such as "Notice the kind of clothes this person is wearing", "Imagine how old you think this person is", etc. All were followed by the same question, "Does that make you feel superior, inferior or equal to this person?" Explanations and justifications for any answer were not allowed; there could only be one answer for each observation. After a time, we switched positions and then partners, until everyone had done the exercise with everyone else in the group.

This exercise was a very powerful demonstration of the way judgments limit our relationships. Many people had difficulty expressing feelings of superiority out loud, even though it was easy for them to feel inferior in front of the group. Many opted to use "equal to" in place of "superior" for fear of appearing conceited, but that kind of thinking defeats the purpose of the exercise. The point of course, is that *any* judgment places limits on your ability to relate to someone. Feeling inferior doesn't help anyone any more than feeling superior does. Feeling equal is just an excuse to hang out with people who are like you. It's a form of cliquish superiority. When we find out later that our equals are actually inferior or superior in some way, we may feel betrayed and move on.

A person may go through an entire life functioning on the basis of stored judgments and trapped feelings. Usually though, there are points throughout life at which a person receives a wake-up call. When the conscious mind has been unable or unwilling to access the spiritual dimension of its being-ness by opening itself to questioning the judgments stored by the subconscious for a very long period of time, the super-conscious usually asserts itself by presenting new challenges. The person may suddenly find himself facing bankruptcy after years of financial independence. A family member may experience a sudden and tragic death. The person may undergo a traumatic personal experience. For many, this comes in the form of something like an accident, having to go through a surgery or being diagnosed with a life-threatening illness. A mid-life crisis is a common way many people begin to question the importance of the things in their lives they had been placing most of their attention on.

We are here to learn about life. This can't be done if you never question anything in your realm of personal truth. We are here to learn how to really live, to experience life in all its feeling splendor, and in doing so, to recognize the universal nature of our collective being-ness. The One recognizes itself in its diversity. It is the mission of diversity is to recognize The One within itself.

Even this description is still limited by dualistic thinking. In the cyclic, spiral nature of creation, exemplified by the helix of strands of biological DNA, the world of matter evolves toward its spiritual nature and upon becoming one with it, begins to separate again to explore further the evolution of its existence. Eventually it becomes one again with its spiritual nature, only to separate again.

You may wonder how long these cycles last. Since time is a creation of the world of matter, the question becomes irrelevant. The amount of time matter and Spirit are One could be a fraction of a second or it could be an eternity. It doesn't really matter to Spirit because the experience of Oneness is so profound it defies the limiting concept of time. We may perceive that it takes eons for matter to evolve completely toward Spirit when experiencing the world of matter, but a brief moment in the bliss of Nirvana or the Kingdom of Heaven removes this concern. This is not to say that suddenly finding yourself back in the world of matter is not a letdown, at least momentarily. But the brief moment of that experience can fill one with enough quiet wisdom and strength to carry through the rest of life with grace and purpose. The One encompasses both the duality and the unity.

Flowing in rhythmic undulation
With the waves, some smaller, some larger,
Some gently caressing,
Some overwhelming in their force,
Washing us ashore as we resurface
While the riptide pulls us under.
They carry us away...

11

Finding Your Niche in a World with One Mission

Getting to that place in life where you feel vibrantly alive, comfortable with your journey and worthy of being here is finding your niche. Finding your niche allows you to not only express your life in a more meaningful way but it contributes to a better quality of life for the entire planet. When you find your piece of the puzzle you make it easier for others to find theirs.

Finding one's niche in life is a challenge for many of us. Although a few child prodigies may be born fully aware of their niche, most of us look around a while. A classic example (pardon the pun) of a child prodigy is Mozart, who began composing music in his very early years.

Some of us go from one thing to the next throughout life, never really settling on just one career, life partner or way of being. Transitioning through many changes can be a kind of niche. These are the gypsies and the mavericks – those who seek personal freedom and self-discovery in a varied lifestyle. For some it's not really a niche, but more

escape from self-examination. For others, it leads to expanded awareness.

One of my closest friends in this life was a man who
was this kind of spiritual maverick, a person whose sense of
personal freedom and invulnerability was unstoppable.
We knew each other for less than a year, yet his presence
had a profound influence on my life. We connected almost
immediately on a spiritual level, a connection that may
seem unlikely since I was a bartender at the time and he was
a salesperson for a car-leasing company. We were both living in Scottsdale, Arizona.

In an earlier part of his life he had been a policeman in
Chicago during the political riots of the late 1960's. He had
war stories to tell. His outgoing and straightforward
manner combined with his blunt honesty and lack of material values fascinated me. He was handsome, magnetic,
arrogant and adventurous all at that same time.

"I'm a high priest" he had told me in confidence
during our second or third meeting. "I know I am divine.
And I'm also a poet and a Viking. I feel the Spirit of being a
Viking within me. I wrote a poem about it. It's part of who
I am. And I'm a holy man." He knew The One and he knew
that it embraced everything. He was unembarrassed to own
the idea of being a ruthless conqueror while at the same
time being passionate, romantic and spiritually inspired.
He felt no contradiction. The Latin Americans have a saying
that resonates along the same lines: "De medico, poeta y
loco, todos tenemos un poco." It means "Physician,
poet and lunatic, we all have a little of each." Greg understood this.

He urged me to read Henry David Thoreau's classic
book *Walden*. In case you haven't read it, it's a nineteenth
century chronicle of Thoreau's experiences while living in a

remote woodland cabin next to Walden Pond in New England while existing as self-sufficiently as possible for two years. It also describes many of his realizations about the nature of existence. Although I had been exposed to the book in college, I had not been receptive enough at that time to be interested in it. This time I devoured it with insight and enthusiasm. I was deeply moved.

After a few weeks of knowing each other he left his job at the car leasing agency and took a job as a cook at a remote camp in northern Arizona just off the Navajo Reservation. He lived in a beat-up old trailer provided to him by the camp he worked for.

I drove the six hours to visit him for a few days and we reveled in the solitude and rustic lifestyle he was enjoying. We spent our evenings leaning against sandstone rocks under the umbrella of a star-studded sky, discussing the ways of the universe while sharing a bottle of wine. During the days we walked around looking at rocks and clouds, made love or sat by the lagoon.

In the weeks that followed we exchanged passionate postcards and poems. Occasionally he would get to a phone booth where he could call me. Even if cell phones had been available back then, they wouldn't have worked in the remote area he was in, fifty miles from the nearest small town and barricaded all around as it was by rocky bluffs. Greg wouldn't have wanted one anyway. Our relationship was odd because although we professed our love for each other, we considered ourselves merely friends, not lovers. His love felt brotherly but not incestuous.

A few months after my visit to see him, I sold most of what I owned at a garage sale and gave notice to quit my job. Greg planned to leave his at the end of the summer season. He came back to Scottsdale and the two of us loaded up what we had left in my Datsun B210 and prepared to head for Colorado. For those who don't remember, the Datsun B210 was a Nissan product - it was the least expensive and tiniest car on the market at the time. Greg was six foot, five inches tall - in addition, I was bringing a seventy-pound dog I had rescued from the humane society just a couple of months earlier. We loaded up the car and put what we couldn't get inside under a tarp on the rooftop carrier. We called it the "blue bubble" and it nearly doubled the height of the car. I guess you get the picture. We left at ten o'clock at night to move to Colorado.

We spent several days camped along a fast-flowing icy mountain stream in a spectacular setting near Telluride. Dinners were lentils or brown rice cooked over a Coleman burner. Evenings we would read aloud from Walt Whitman's *Leaves of Grass* by the light of the campfire. During the day we would walk several miles to a roadside store to purchase a few sundries or a six-pack of beer. We didn't need ice because we could chill our drinks in the mountain stream, which also served for bathing and drinking water.

After a while we moved on and camped near Durango, where we hoped there would be more opportunity for employment. We met a guy who offered to let us stay at his place for a while. He seemed friendly enough but after living there a few days I was unnerved by his collection of guns, mercenary magazines and tendency to go off on psychotic rants about the government. Greg, as usual, was unflappable.

I managed to find a tiny, worn-out old trailer for rent, not much better than the one Greg had lived in during his months as a cook in northern Arizona, and used most of what I had saved to get moved in. We lived there for a couple of months. I got a job at the local Holiday Inn as a bartender and he got temporary work with a local rancher. Since he had moved to Colorado with no car and only forty dollars in his pocket, he either had to hitchhike to work or I had to take him.

When his work for the rancher ended, Greg moved on to nearby Farmington, New Mexico, where he was trying to get a job working the gas and oil fields. We parted close friends but decided not to keep track of each other. It was a "leave it to the universe" sort of attitude. I chanced to see him one more time.

I was with a new man several months later and happened to see him walking down the street in Farmington as we drove by. The man I was with, who would later become my second husband, agreeably stopped so I could talk to Greg. The three of us had a drink at a nearby bar. He brought me up to speed. He had lived in the back of a pick-up with a topper for a couple weeks that he had borrowed from one of the "roughnecks" at his job in the oil fields. After he had earned enough money, he had purchased the truck for three hundred dollars and lived in it for a few more weeks. The weather was turning cold when the truck was taken away from him. Apparently the owner he bought it from did not have clear title when he signed it over.

Yet Greg's attitude had been philosophic. "For three hundred dollars I had transportation and a place to stay for a while. I knew something else would come along." And it had. Greg was living with a new girl and still working the oil fields. He was working on getting together some money to buy another vehicle. After that, who knows? Maybe Montana? The atmosphere was congenial and accepting. Greg smiled warmly at my new friend and told him, "She's a great lady" without the slightest hint of possessiveness or regret. The three of us had an enjoyable talk and I never saw him again. Yet Greg and I both knew that our presence in each other's lives had been powerful and profound.

In later years I often wondered how he was or what he was doing. I sometimes regretted that we hadn't kept in touch. But I also realized that his chapter in my life was a special part of my journey that didn't require follow-up to validate its importance. And I knew he could take care of himself. "I'm a survivor," he would say. "I'll always get by."

His trust in the universe was absolute. And he was completely confident of his place within it. He had no shame of himself and no judgment of others. The world was his theater, and its drama was his entertainment. Because he saw himself in everyone, he achieved instant rapport. And that, combined with his easy acceptance of the way things were, seemed to always make things work out for him.

Most of us will not find our niche in quite such a laissez-faire attitude. Most of us feel an urge deep within to pursue some project, activity or career that feels personally rewarding or right to us. Finding your niche is fulfilling your life mission in your own unique way. It is a way that brings you greater appreciation and awareness of the present. It strengthens your sense of self-esteem. And it fulfills you.

Finding your niche is a matter of opening up to what you want in your heart. To know what you want in your heart, you must be able to feel what it's trying to tell you. To be able to feel it you must remove the judgments surrounding your experiences.

Many begin finding their niche at midlife. Some have known their niche all along but let their filtered perceptions of how one should live get in the way. This is the cause of the classic mid-life crisis. A person goes through life accord-ing to the perceived values that are assimilated throughout early life. When life no longer seems as if it will go on forever, or the person faces a traumatic change in lifestyle, a mid-life crisis is triggered, causing the person to re-evaluate priorities.

For example, let's say you are now working at a job that pays well enough to offer some financial stability. Let's say you are a department supervisor at a marketing firm. It's easy for you because you've been in the business a long time and you know your work backward and forward. Co-workers and the clients you work with acknowledge and accept your position within the work environment and business world. The work is familiar to you and you are comfortable with it.

Yet deep inside you really want to do something else. You know you would really rather be working on that idea for a video documentary you've had in mind for a number of years, but you can't seem to find the time. You fantasize about doing it but it never materializes. You haven't made it a priority. You have too many judgments that prevent you from making the change:

"It would be irresponsible to just quit my job and do that."

"I don't have time to work it in, and I can't quit what I'm doing now until there's enough money to do it."

"It would be selfish."

"I'm not good enough at that."

"I don't have the connections."

"Life was never meant to be easy."

Your mind will continue to come up with reasons why you should never change what you are doing because what you are doing is familiar, even if it's not working for you financially or providing a sense of personal fulfillment. The subconscious aspect of mind loves what is familiar. It is the great storehouse of the familiar, a virtual library of information recording every memory, every learning experience, every emotion and every bit of data you have ever been exposed to that could be used as a benchmark against which to gauge the present or to fertilize your imagination at any time, now or in the future.

Years go by and suddenly you realize life is getting behind you. The years ahead don't seem to offer unlimited opportunities for procrastination anymore. Your energy level is not what it used to be and you notice the skin of your face and neck beginning to sag. Yet you continue to do the same thing, mindlessly hoping that something will come along to change your world for you.

The super-conscious mind, which inspires from a more trans-dimensional awareness, keeps pushing us to change in spite of ourselves. It plants the seeds of restlessness that desire to know more, to become more.

Then one day something happens. You get a phone call with some devastating news that shakes your world. Or maybe you find yourself in bed recovering from an accident or sudden health crisis. And then your world does begin to change. You begin to re-evaluate all your priorities. You realize the niche you've been filling feels more like a sinkhole than a position from which to explore your talents and interests. Spirit has stirred within you and awakened you to the messages of your heart. You realize it's time to get going. The value of being alive has taken on a new and greater importance. You begin to search for more meaning in the things you do every day. The seeds of restlessness have finally begun to sprout and grow back toward the light.

Suddenly the compost of life's past experience stored in the subconscious mind becomes the fertilizer for the newly sprouted seeds pushing to the surface of conscious awareness. By releasing judgments attached to past experiences, the experiences themselves become fertilizer for a richer life. By releasing judgments about what self is feeling, compassion for all takes its place. Like a flower shooting up through compost, it is often through the rotting decay of an emotional wasteland that the blossom of Spirit asserts itself.

But why wait to be bombarded with change in such a cataclysmic way when you have the option to go for it right now with less stress? Your super-conscious Spirit has been nudging you along already. If it were not, you probably wouldn't be reading this book.

I have said many times that we are all one mind. As such we all have one mission. The mission is to become fully aware of who we are as omnipotent, omniscient, omnipresent spiritual beings manifesting the glory and power of The One. We do this by starting on an individual level. As aspects of the One that have differentiated into identities that see themselves as separate, we must begin by looking within ourselves for our personal truth in order to discover our personal path within the mission. Once we have discovered and released enough judgments to feel the essence of our beings, relief, forgiveness and healing replace anxiety, guilt and blame.

Then an interesting thing happens. We begin to want to share these new feelings with others. We begin to want to help others along the way, as we have been helped. This new way of being is a compassionate self that sees itself in the pain and struggle of others. And thus, the drive for healing continues on a more expanded level.

At this point we often try to tell others how to help themselves. We rely on our own experience and think that should be good enough to help them along. Then we don't understand when they do not seem to get it the same way we do.

It's a little like parents not wanting to see their children make the same mistakes they did. They may do everything differently than their own parents did, hoping the child will not make the same mistakes. They may try to control every aspect of the child's existence, smothering originality and the willingness to explore and take chances. What often happens is the child ends up with completely different problems and challenges the parent is not equipped to deal with.

Just as children learn best when guided to learn from experiences themselves, rather than having everything done for them or by being tightly controlled, adults also need to have their own spiritual awakenings and personal realizations. To become aware of and integrate their power, people need to learn their own lessons. They do best when guided to discover personal truth for themselves, rather than being told what personal truth is. Personal truth is just that – personal.

Even though we are all ultimately One awareness, the differentiated aspects of our various identities must discover that connection within our differentiated hearts, each in our own way, in our own time. The best we can do is to be the best we can be.

Personal growth and spiritual healing is the first and most important step anyone can take toward healing the problems of the world. It begins by examining, without judging and in an impeccably honest way, the contents of your own heart. You must know yourself deeply and profoundly. From there it is a matter of seeing opportunities to help others as the opportunities present themselves and as you are able to act on them. This is the seed of the mission each person is born into the world with. The path to personal growth and fulfillment is the only path that truly helps others in anything more than a superficial way. Paradoxically and in a symbiotic way, only by helping others can we find lasting peace and fulfillment, but the journey inward must come first.

Finding a way to express your life mission that feels right is a matter of finding your niche. Your niche is the means to express your mission in the world in a way that feels natural and right to you. It is most easily accomplished when you find your right livelihood. Your right livelihood is a way of making a living that utilizes your natural talents and interests. Work is enjoyable because you are doing something you love.

You give the world a great gift when you show up for who you are. Come from your heart, not from what you think others believe or expect. Discover what makes you feel excited about life. When you have clarity about a vision or goal you would like to manifest, you attract the power to create it within your life. Obstacles fall away. What you focus on is drawn to you. By creating authentic meaning in your life you add value to the planet.

People that are crippled by the smothering of their personal truth do not have the free attention or focus necessary to create what they really want. Because they have not been open to examining what lies within them, they live according to the real or imagined expectations of an anonymous and ubiquitous "them".

Your resistance toward finding your niche and living your mission is based on a fear of the unknown. The subconscious mind loves familiarity. Remember, its job is to store information, emotions and habits for future reference. Your fear is the story you tell yourself that keeps you in the same place. Continuing to live by your story will shut you down. Finding your niche and moving toward your vision will cause you to feel fulfilled.

Open up to your heart. Remove the judgments surrounding your experiences. Let go of the judgments you hold onto so fiercely about yourself. Know what you want by feeling what your heart is trying to tell you. Know the clarity of a pure moment of being. I promise you, the rewards are infinitely greater than you may have come to expect.

The ocean of emotion is
Sometimes gently caressing,
Sometimes overwhelming in its force.
It carries me away…
It takes me home.

12

The Gatekeepers

If the body is the temple of the soul, the mind and emotions are its gatekeepers. All illness and health, strength and weakness, beauty and disfigurement of the body are manifestations of soul intention filtered through the individual's personality of beliefs, perspectives and emotional disposition.

For example, Spirit may decide that it wishes to experience the effects of a debilitating illness and its accompanying feelings of helplessness, such as in the case of ALS (Lou Gherig's disease). This experience will be perceived uniquely by the person having it according to the emotional and mental configuration of his inner world. Some will surrender to the disease in self-pity while others will begin to appreciate what life they have left. Some will surrender gracefully and take the time to reflect soulfully. Still others will resist it entirely, becoming demanding and bitter. It is possible the afflicted may experience a bit of all of these along the way. Disease is not always graceful or dignified but has much to teach us about ourselves. Sometimes the person who is ill becomes the teacher of the well, other times the illness instructs the sick. Sometimes the lessons are overlooked.

Death can be a healing. And sometimes it's the catalyst for someone close to the person who passed on to be healed emotionally. The people in the environment surrounding the one with the illness have decided on a super-conscious level to participate in some way in the experience of this person's illness. The purpose may be to learn what it feels like to give help unconditionally or to simply begin to appreciate one's own experience of each passing day in a richer way. Each person's experience of the situation will be directed by personal viewpoints, beliefs and the level of self-esteem. If a person is overcome by resentment about the circumstances, it will be difficult to feel what the experience can offer on a spiritual level.

Calamity and harmony, stress and relaxation, happiness and sadness, excitement and boredom are all reflections of the perceptions and beliefs of the person experiencing them. Beliefs are thought forms that are often based on emotional experiences of the past. They attract the circumstances of the reality you find yourself in now.

As humans we tend to have an egoic need to be right - even beliefs formed as a result of processing circumstantial evidence that is not emotionally charged may be difficult to change, simply because the ego's need to be right is emotionally charged. I sometimes think of the EGO as an acronym for Emotions Going Out-of-control. Until the universe delivers evidence to support a new belief, it is supported only by your faith in it. Once the evidence is there, changing beliefs is more difficult unless you realize that beliefs are always a choice.

If there is a lack of evidence or conviction the believer may seek out like-minded people for validation. If there are unrecognized subconscious beliefs that conflict with a belief one intends to embrace, that person may give up on the belief before it can manifest the corresponding reality it would otherwise attract.

Many of these beliefs exist in the form of judgments, which is what gives them their emotional power to attract undesired circumstances. The way to discover these judgments is to follow the buried treasure of feelings to their source. The more powerful the emotional charge pertaining to a belief, the more readily it will attract experience that bears it out, positively or negatively. If you want something very badly but there is more negative emotion around the idea of not having it than there is confidence in your ability to manifest it, the unwanted experience will win out.

There is no experience that does not have value for Spirit. It is only our judgments and perceptions that limit us in the spiritual growth that could be gained from them. Experience is the great tattle-tale of our judgments and prejudices. It reveals our personal truth to the world, a fact the ego does not always want to embrace. Behind each challenging experience Spirit is watching patiently, waiting for the mind and emotions to let go enough to allow the experience in a non-judgmental way. Feelings are pure experience, but when feelings are infected with judgments, they limit the ability of the person feeling them to move through the experience in a way that is helpful to Spirit. The infection of judgments creates dis-ease, literally a lack of ease with life, that may later manifest as physical disease. The human experience is a channel for Spirit, in sickness as well as health. It is the container, the vessel, through which Spirit experiences while on the earth plane.

Being fully empowered includes the ability to see yourself in everyone without judgment. This leads to humility and compassion, self-forgiveness, a feeling of oneness with others and a sense of divine grace. There is no longer anything to fear or resist. The irony is this: that which we most fear is the key to our empowerment. Liberation lies across the threshold of fear.

Life is to experience. The unlimited ground of being from which all creation arises is the experiencer of all its creation. This is what some call God and what I refer to as The One. The divine spark within each Spirit focuses on particular aspects of existence in order to understand them experientially. This is the nature of feeling. When individualized identities forget their connection to The One, experiences are resisted and continue to play out over and over.

When a person realigns with his or her inherent divinity, the judgments surrounding painful or negative circumstances dissolve. Like a river, the Spirit of life moves onward, no longer held back in the reservoir of resisted experience, flowing naturally to eventually join the ocean of expanded awareness. We must learn to let go so that life may flow like a river. When a resisted experience is allowed to run its course and a person really involves himself in the feeling of it without judging it, there is no need to repeat it. New frontiers of possibility open up. This cannot occur when a person's ability to manifest what they want is tied up in the resistance of unwanted experiences.

To unleash your creative power you must begin where you are now. Notice the prejudices in your particular view of the world. Pay attention to the assumptions you make about people and situations based on past experience. What are you feeling? Are you numb? Even numbness is a feeling. Like sitting frozen in one position too long, when the emotional body starts to move, it will experience pain and discomfort for a while when a different position is taken. At first the movements will be stiff and uncomfortable – you didn't realize how much your position had cut off feeling in a certain area, but after a while, movement becomes natural again. The soul is similar to the body in this way. We are not designed to stay in one position too long!

Like the body, feelings need to move. Attempting to block undesired feelings or hang on desperately to feelings of joy or happiness only halts the flow of the life force, and the reservoir begins to fill and stagnate.

The creative force that permeates every aspect of our universe as well as the unmanifest is not a static force. Due to its creative nature it must continually experiment. This is soul evolution. The One experiences through the myriad wonders of its created universes. If this were not so there would be nothing to perceive or experience, only the great Void of unlimited potential out of which all creation arose, a pure vacuum. The essence of the divine *is* this great Void, a random infinity of creative potential. Creation is the organization and manifestation of certain aspects of this potential through the power of intention. These aspects are actually indescribable because their very definition is an act of creation and the Void has no definition. It exists everywhere, within and outside of everything, potent with possibility. It is less than nothing, yet it is everything. It is so vacuous that it draws everything toward itself. This is the draw of Spirit calling its created aspects home. Through the power of creation the cycle repeats itself.

Have you ever noticed how when you use a vacuum cleaner, the machine doesn't just suck in air? It also blows it out at the opposite end. This is how the Void (infinite possibility) and Creation (manifestation) inter-relate. The Void draws creation back into itself, back home. Creation erupts from the limitless potential that is the emptiness. Movement is cyclic, like the symbol for infinity that looks like a sideways figure eight. Yet even to define it in this way places limits on it. If you believe in the idea of the Big Bang

Theory of creation, you might say we are still riding the currents of that explosion, eventually to be drawn home again. Out of the infinite quiet of divine potential The One created all, including mental and emotional planes, parallel universes, the magical and mundane and anything else you can think of that exists or does not exist.

The One experiences through these manifestations, and people, created in the image and likeness of The One, experience through manifestations arising out of their own beliefs, intentions, judgments and resistances. The One's desire to experience in human form is an ongoing experiment, made more interesting by the diversification and individualization of free will. But The One is patient. We each discover the ramifications of our expressions of free will and individual choice in our own time and in our own way. At times we sense the divine and move closer through love and compassion, at others we increase our separation by making judgments that resist the fullness of experience.

We must learn to be patient with ourselves, but not quit trying. Spirit yearns to move to a higher level of awareness. So much has been written about it. The origins of all great religions were inspired by insights into the nature of this ultimate reality, yet it cannot be defined in terms the intellect can easily grasp. Versions have been articulated in a variety of ways by vastly different persons in touch with it so that others may intuitively sense its truth, even if they do not yet have sufficient understanding to embody this awareness. Much inspired religious literature conveys information that has been misinterpreted or poorly translated to make it more palatable to the masses. In many cases the messengers – the religious leaders and translators – simply did not have "eyes to see" or "ears to hear" the feeling experience behind the words. The essence, the mystical aspect, of the message was watered down or completely changed. It is important to intuit the feelings behind the words. Words alone are insufficient and judgments will cloud the intuition. Feel.

A mystic or a saint speaks with a conviction that comes from knowing this higher ground from personal experience. His presence is so inspiring that others are converted or transformed by his teachings even if they do not fully understand them. They *feel* the truth. This feeling creates a faith that has strength and creative power. Faith arises from an inner conviction of the truth of one's beliefs and gives hope and resilience in times of trial and suffering. It helps to conquer fear, which is the absence of love. When fear is conquered, love can pour forth into one's being. When one embodies love, there is no more need to prove anything to anyone. The person is living in a state of grace, the higher . ground of a more expanded awareness.

For a long time I was in such hot pursuit of my spiritual path that I forgot to live. I was so concerned about where I was going that I forgot where I was. I was restless and discontented but still thought of myself as a seeker. Do you understand the problem here? I might have been happier if I could have just thought of myself as a spiritual being. My belief was that I was a "seeker". The reality it created was that I was always seeking, never finding. I did not know how to "just be". I didn't like what I felt inside so I certainly did not want to be that. I didn't realize that the key to opening up to Spirit was by feeling whatever was already inside of me. It certainly wasn't very glamorous or spiritual sounding. My beingness was clouded by judgments about who I was. I had the idea I should just transcend it all, which of course, created resistance to whatever was there in the first place.

Your higher self has chosen things for you to experience and learn from, and these are not always the same experiences the ego would choose. Experience what is in front of you right now. Resistances and judgments to an experience obscure the purity of the moment. To get past this, you must first recognize the judgments for what they are, and begin to notice the impact they are having on your perceptions. When you can experience something unpleasant without making judgments about yourself, others or life in general, you have opened to the possibility of creating a new, more enjoyable life for yourself.

Happiness is an art form. It does not just happen. You are responsible for the life you are leading, with all its prejudices, judgments and filtered perceptions, as well as its thrills, moments of euphoria and satisfaction.

Each day is a blank canvas upon which to paint. Will you create something fascinating and beautiful today? Your life is a work in progress. Are you creating a masterpiece? Henry David Thoreau said it very succinctly in a passage in his book *Walden*: "It is something to be able to paint a particular picture...but it is far more glorious to carve and paint the very atmosphere and medium through which we look. To affect the quality of the day, that is the highest of arts. Every man is tasked to make his life, even in its details, worthy of the contemplation of his most elevated and critical hour."

Major religions in the world have a legacy of spiritual leaders who were or are able to hear the voice of divine guidance. In Judaism and Christianity, for example, the only thing that made Noah, Abraham or Moses different from anyone else was that they courageously listened to the inner voice of Spirit, even amidst the doubt or criticism of others. Buddha was born a prince into a wealthy family but disregarded the path that was given to him by others in favor of listening to his own inner guidance. He found enlightenment.

In order to develop our creative power in manifesting a life we enjoy we must first surrender to the life we have already created through the ignorance of not knowing ourselves deeply. It is a little like surrendering to what some call the will of God, except that here you are recognizing your part in creating the life you are living through your beliefs, expectations, judgments and unconscious drives and embracing your creative power to change them. In Genesis of the Bible it is stated that God created man and woman in his own image and gave them free will. This free will is the creative force that directs the course of each individual's life, whether shaped through societal and family influences or consciously and deliberately chosen.

Many times people, especially teen-agers, think they are behaving independently and out of choice when they are simply reacting to some societal constraint they don't like. Going against something is not as satisfying or empowering as making a clear and unfettered choice, but both will yield a creative result. Life forms itself around such choices. Realities are as limited or unlimited as the beliefs, imaginations and perceptions of the persons experiencing them.

When a person begins to recognize how his beliefs in the form of judgments are affecting his perceptions of reality and influencing the outcome of his life, it is a time of great reckoning within the soul. The creative force of Spirit manifests one's intentions, however unconscious they may be. Until those results are surrendered to, that is, experienced without judging them or oneself, it is impossible to move forward into a larger arena of possibility. Your power is already tied up in resisting what you don't want to experience.

The power of "going with the flow" is that resisted experience can finally be integrated, opening up new possibilities. Sounds ironic, doesn't it? To increase your ability to create your life as you want it, you must first surrender to the life you already have. This is where feeling and emotion emerge as tools for transformation. Discovering the judgments that create emotional imbalance and surrendering to the flow of feelings allows movement toward an ocean of greater awareness and creative ability. New vistas of possibility open up to the imagination, while simultaneously one may feel deeply saddened at the extent to which self-imposed limitations have been placed. Surrendering to this flow invites the experience of grace.

It is important to be gentle with yourself. It is like awakening from a deep sleep. At first you become aware of your environment, your eyes open and you begin to stretch, moving gradually into the change from sleeping to wakefulness. Occasionally, a person may be jolted out of his spiritual slumber by a traumatic or life-changing experience, like an alarm clock set for a certain time period in life. The awakening may be sudden and disorienting, even life-threatening.

Once awakened within a body and mind, a soul does not easily to go back to sleep. The emotional power of the experience creates a curiosity within the mind that tends to keep it open to new perspectives in its search to find a way back home. If Spirit does not continue to expand within the body, the person will become restless and agitated. Not much is required by Spirit to keep moving, only the continued flow of attention and feeling in the present moment, unclouded by judgments that inhibit clear passage through an experience.

The age-old battle between good and evil is nothing more than an unconscious attempt by the human aspect of self to transcend the duality of life and achieve oneness. Books and movies usually cater to an audience that doesn't understand this oneness, an audience that thinks evil is something to be defeated. Evil must be integrated because it is impossible to defeat. This integration is accomplished by the power of repentance, forgiveness and the desire to make amends and serve others - to achieve spiritual re-connection with The One.

In movies there is also a fascination with the idea of death. You can hardly avoid noticing that the most popular movies today involve a considerable amount of death. Death is something concrete we can observe, but only from the outside. We cannot understand it. The only way to understand death is to experience it firsthand. We are reluctant to go there because we do not have the knowledge while in physical form of how to come back, should we choose to. It is a great unknown. The uniqueness of each person's perspective in life will create a death experience that is unique to that person. We don't get to share in that. It belongs to the dying person alone.

Death is an important part of the great mystery while we are in a body. The word "mystery" means having a quality of being mystical. It has a mystical quality that can't be understood with the rational mind. It is a purely experiential spiritual experience. Death is our return to the source of our experience. Considering how afraid many people are of their divinity, their mystical nature, it is no wonder there is a fear of death among so many. We know intuitively that at death we must face the great mystery alone.

The Obsession

It was her obsession with abstinence and endurance
That seemed unhealthy,
As if the world didn't have enough to go around,
And certainly one as undeserving as she
Could not assume the right to a fair share of it,
So she resigned herself to suffering in hardship and
thoughtless toil,
Hoping that somehow sacrifice and self-denial
Would bring deferred gratification,
A redemption from the judgments of her shortcomings
That caused her to continually bear the burden,
Hailing the Protestant work ethic as her flagship
In hope of some future reward she didn't quite understand,
So that by acknowledging her unworthiness
And withholding satisfaction from herself
She would be allowed space on earth in the meantime,
All the while fearing death.

13

Integrity & Self-Love

Integrity is about maintaining quality and goodwill in one's life. There can only be true integrity when there is no attempt to deceive, not only others, but oneself. By being true to yourself you tune in to your higher purpose. You can only be true to yourself if you are first honest with yourself. Honesty with yourself breeds integrity born of forgiveness and compassion. A life lived in true integrity is the greatest gift one can give the world. Love for humanity and all of creation begins with loving a single individual: yourself. This is where integrity begins.

Loving yourself completely is an absolute prerequisite to serving others with genuine integrity. What is called selfless service is only selfless, can only be selfless, when the need of the person for self-acceptance has been satisfied. This is not an egoic thing. The lack of self-acceptance in a person whose heart is full of self-judgments, self-criticisms and un-integrated emotional fragments will prevent service to others from being as beneficial to the collective mind as it could be. Heal yourself first, then you can more effectively assist others in your universe. Love yourself uncondition-

ally and you will discover genuine compassion and acceptance for others. Your complete self-acceptance is a gift to the
cosmos.

When love of self is freed from negative self-talk and
judgments, the world becomes less threatening and more
loving, your vision becomes transformed and life becomes
interesting and joyful. The fear of trying something new
becomes an excitement to see what will happen if you do.

When self-love is present and you experience judgments or negative feelings directed toward you by someone
else, you can appreciate their lack of integration as a reflection of their lack of self-love and experience compassion in
the recognition. *You know what it is like.*

When your own cup is full you will be able to share
the overflow with others. Until you love yourself, your
actions toward others will be tainted by neediness and a
desire to manipulate their lives in a way that serves only
you. There can be no compassion when self-love is not
part of one's reality. There can be sympathy, pity and even
camaraderie, but not compassion. Compassion for others
arises out of honest and intense self-examination, including
a non-judgmental awareness and appreciation for oneself
and one's feelings. Life becomes holy. Every feeling experience becomes sacred in its contribution to the growth of the
soul. Life becomes an active meditation and the world
becomes one's temple.

The more you allow yourself to feel, the more your
self-acceptance generates personal magnetism. The more
you love yourself, the more compassion you feel for those
around you. The biggest reason people have trouble loving
one another is a lack of self-love.

If self-love is not ego-centered but based on an authentic sense of worthiness unfettered by negative memories of

past experiences, love and compassion for all of humanity will naturally flow forth. You will begin to appreciate the diversity of human expression and experience. You will be able to relate to others because you see yourself in them. You begin to do this by feeling whatever it is you feel on the inside, without judging it.

By appreciating the diversity of your emotional repertoire you become more authentic, more you. This doesn't mean you will be faced with a life of riding an emotional roller coaster. That is what you have been doing, but you have been doing it strapped in by the seat belt of judgment. If you let go of the restraining judgments and take that wild ride you will discover the clear space of inner peace that lies beyond it.

When you honestly give validation to your emotional expression you are telling your subconscious mind that it is okay to be who you are and feel the way you feel. This does not mean blaming yourself or others. You simply allow yourself to feel the way you do until the feeling has run itself out. Harboring a grudge or blaming someone else for your attitude assigns your personal power to the source of your blame. There is no flow of emotion because feelings are stuck in the mire of judgments. Because feelings are stuck they try to escape any way possible, usually by negative, self-defeating and destructive thought habits. These habits eventually take on a life of their own and appear to operate without your intention or permission. They assert themselves whenever they are triggered by anything similar that reminds them of the judgment that caused them to resist feeling something. The mind justifies its stuck-ness by telling you that you are "controlling" emotions. What is happening is that the emotions are controlling the mind. The mind thinks emotions are too messy, but it is the mind that has created the mess by adding judgments to feelings.

Emotions are created out of feelings biased by the non-accepting, judgmental attitudes of the mind. Emotions require acceptance by the mind in the form of quiet observation. You must first drop the judgments and simply feel what is there. The synergy between mind and feeling requires feelings to be accepted by the mind in order to flow freely. The mental body needs this free flow in order to avoid becoming cluttered with damaging thought patterns that limit its efficiency and ability to create what is truly desired in one's life. Recognizing judgments and dropping them allows the flow to begin.

An egotistical or conceited kind of self-love is really insecurity. A desire to assert one's superiority always derives from a deep sense of powerlessness and lack of self-worth, however well hidden.

True self-love is humble and content. A person who loves herself recognizes her weaknesses. She sees herself in the weaknesses of others. She feels the intensity of her experiences but does not judge herself for feelings. She regards mistakes and poor choices as learning tools for creating a more enjoyable reality. She can suffer criticism and gossip without losing her self-esteem. In the face of anger she can remain calm and appreciative of the other person's viewpoint. If she doesn't, she immediately forgives herself.

This kind of self-love arises out of a deep sense of security. The world no longer appears threatening. The faults of others are viewed with compassion and a sense of unity.

If you make peace with the inner self, you will feel a connectedness with all others that allows you to rejoice in their choices and accomplishments as if they were your own. A surprising thing happened when I started to re-own qualities I saw in others that I had projected outward because I didn't like them in myself. I began to re-own the disowned magnificence I had also projected out into the world! You can use the concept of a mirror to see aspects of yourself in someone whom you deem to have greater talents or qualities than you. Thank him in your mind for his wonderful attributes. Identify with him and feel into a quality you appreciate. Enjoy his successes and triumphs vicariously. Honor and appreciate the fact that someone is manifesting that particular quality of human consciousness. Feel your connection to him through the wireless network of the collective mind that senses our unity as One. Enjoy your perception of him. Feel gratitude for the presence he brings to the world, for the gift of his talent or accomplishment or for simply being who he is. You are appreciating an aspect of The One that we exist with as co-creators. It is perfectly okay to enjoy it! Cheer at the triumph of others and feel your connection to them. Thrill in the connection by experiencing vicariously through them. We are One.

The modern day idolatry of rock stars and movie icons is a demonstration of that kind of connection, but on an unconscious level. In this case we have projected our magnificence outward. As a society we are collectively grateful and appreciative of their ability to act out aspects of ourselves that we feel and desire but feel we cannot, for whatever reason, express. We express our gratitude by giving them massive doses of attention and paying money to see them perform. What most of us don't realize is that they are mirrors of ourselves. Whether you resent them, feel jealous of them or adore them, there is something there for you to look at.

Feelings of a lack of self-worth are nearly universal and are based on a fear of enlightenment, or re-connecting to one's own divinity. It seems to be deeply etched into the collective mind, exemplified by the classic Old Testament description of Adam and Eve's fall from grace in the Garden of Eden. What history has called the "fall of man" was such a traumatic experience for the collective mind that there is still a great deal of resistance around the idea of opening to and embracing one's own divinity. The fear of punishment for doing so is a fear of having to go back to a more unenlightened state, of being "cast from the garden". Before eating the forbidden fruit which contained the knowledge of good and evil, the couple did not know a dualistic existence. They knew only their divine nature as an aspect of The One. Once they became aware of and began to live in duality they could no longer exist in their divine unity.

Each day we continue to eat the forbidden fruit when we perceive things around us as good and evil. Transcendence of this dualistic way of thinking by dropping judgments is what returns us to the Void, even if only momentarily. The more time spent in the quietness of the Void, the greater our abilities become to create something truly wonderful through our recognition of ourselves as aspects of The One.

Love sets no limitations on its growth or ability to change.
That which comes from the heart
Does not need to bind itself to be true.
It needs to be free to express what is.
Feeling anew the freshness of love not taken for granted,
A love not due to force or obligation
Is the ultimate freedom.

14

The Freedom of Self-Love

Love does conquer all. Love embodies all, even fear. Love sets our Spirits free. Love tames the challenges of living and fills one with compassion for all of humanity. It exudes an appreciation for everything that exists. When we are filled with love, we are in touch with our divine nature. I am not talking about romantic or familial love. That is a connection of kindred souls who have chosen to work through certain experiences together while incarnate in order to learn from these experiences. The kind of love I am referring to is compassionate toward all of creation, a love that does not feel judgments toward those who are on a different path.

The voice of Spirit is as diverse as the people who hear it. No two paths to The One are alike and each hears the voice of Spirit in his or her own way. When the mind is in a state of passive receptivity Spirit can be heard. This is the way a small child sees the world. Everything is fascinating and new.

Learning to embody this unconditional love is the purpose of our migrations in the human realm and re-unites us with our divine nature. Our purpose is to experience The One incarnate. It is what the spiritual master Jesus embodied, and told us we all can do. Most of us have experienced flashes of insight or moments of grace when we intuitively knew this to be true. All struggle and suffering is a result of separation from this knowing. Remembering it keeps the thread of faith firmly connected from our day-to-day consciousness to the formless ground of divine Oneness. Once we have remembered who we truly are we can be effective in our secondary purpose: to assist others in the process of remembering their divine origin.

While Jesus of Nazareth was incarnate he said there were just two commandments we needed to observe to lead a spiritual life. The first was to love God with heart, soul, strength and mind (feeling, spiritual, physical and mental aspects). This is the call of Spirit to remember itself as The One while experiencing in the physical plane.

The second commandment is about self-love: love your neighbor as yourself. Many have mistaken this to mean that we should place the importance of others above ourselves. Our most important spiritual task is to tend to the evolution of the soul in the particular incarnation we are in. We cannot do this for another in a direct way, as everyone has free will. We can only do it for ourselves. By tending to your own soul evolution you automatically assist others to do the same by your effect on the collective mind. If your needs as a total being (heart, soul, strength and mind) are unfulfilled and you attempt to teach or perform charity for others, your gifts will be tainted by your sense of unworthiness. Until one has learned to love oneself unconditionally, it just isn't possible to love others that way.

It's only natural to love, honor and protect the aspect of The One that you are currently manifesting. It is your sacred duty to remove it from danger and to encourage this aspect of Oneness (what you think of as yourself) to learn and grow. Your "self" is your holy responsibility and it is healthy to cherish it. Hate yourself, judge yourself, and you will express this as hatred and judgments toward others. Love yourself truly, deeply and unconditionally and you will experience genuine empathy and caring for the concerns of others, as well as acceptance of their short-comings.

When Jesus said to love your neighbor as yourself he was speaking quite literally. "Love your neighbor as yourself" is not just a nice idea. The way we give or withhold love to those around us is a mirror of the way we feel about ourselves. The world is your mirror. If we are loathing ourselves for all our faults and not forgiving ourselves for our perceived shortcomings, we are doing the same thing to others in our lives. Jesus did not say to love your neighbor more than yourself, but as yourself. He recognized the one-ness of our collective consciousness and the reflective nature of our interactions. Loving and forgiving yourself is a favor to the world, because it frees you up to embrace life and gives you the ability to love others unconditionally too. Many of us have grown up being taught that it's vain and egotistical, even sinful, to love ourselves. But when your own cup is empty, how can you share it with another?

If you love yourself completely and allow yourself the fullness of your feelings and experiences, you will find your cup running over with the richness of life. Wanting to help others will be the result of a heartfelt desire to share this richness with others. You will love others as yourself because you can see yourself in everyone. As you see your-self in the shortcomings of others, you experience humility. As you see yourself in their triumphs, you experience euphoria. As you forgive yourself for your shortcomings, you easily forgive others. As you learn to love yourself completely you feel compassion for others. We are all One. We are The One. When you feel the truth of this you will know what it means to love your neighbor as yourself.

What we all need first before we can be of any real service to the rest of the world is to love ourselves. All attempts to put others first, to serve others, etc., are a depletion of the life force if self-love is not realized first. Usually these acts of service are masqueraded attempts to feel better about self by trying to use service to others as a means of healing emotional pain. It is finding reasons to love yourself. If you heal yourself first - by forgiving everyone in your universe, including yourself, for shortcomings and feeling a genuine sense of your intrinsic worthiness – your desire to serve will be motivated to help others share the inner peace you now know. It will be truly selfless. Selfless service is an act that optimally benefits the collective mind. It lays the groundwork for cooperation rather than competition, empowering others rather than dominating them and eases the suffering of others by the presence of an empathy arising from an intuitive connection with the collective mind.

To understand this you must have an open mind. You must be open to loving yourself with all of your faults. You must be open to admitting to yourself that the things that drive you crazy in others are reflections of your disowned personality fragments. When you re-own these personality fragments, you become more whole, more unified. This unity, because it contains all possibilities, contributes to unity among humankind. When others realize their wholeness in the expression of multiple facets of the human condition and sense these facets as aspects of a greater whole, humanity has moved closer to unity.

Like facets on a gemstone, the expression of a person's life is a gem that reflects many facets. The variations in color, shape and reflectiveness vary according to the perspective from which they are viewed. They glitter differently as life expresses itself through the turn of events and people's reactions to them. Just as a gemstone reflects different dimensions in its rotation under the light of a store display window, life reflects back to us many varied possibilities, reflections and expressions, depending upon our perspective at the point of perception.

As tools of The One in its purpose to experience manifest life forms, we are each expressions of uniqueness. How we choose to use that uniqueness is what determines the level of satisfaction in our lives. If love and service to others is truly selfless, there is no sense of loss or sacrifice. There is only the gratitude of being able to assist others to find more joy and inner peace. Selflessness cannot be accomplished without intense self-examination culminating in a forgiving self-acceptance. When a person operates out of complete self-acceptance it includes embracing the processes currently going on in one's life. These processes include relationships, living situations, level of health and prosperity and so forth. Self-love includes being able to say "no" and not feel guilty about it.

Self-love also includes taking the time and space necessary to replenish your inner reserves. This downtime includes getting enough sleep, taking time for reflection and contemplation and pursuing personal hobbies that excite or energize you. A suitable personal hobby could be anything that makes you feel energized, excited or content when you do it. It could be bird-watching, hiking, stamp collecting, fishing, sports, quilting or any other activity that lets you forget yourself. Many people favor artistic expression or writing.

Replenishing your inner reserves includes self-improvement, whether in a class or through private study.

It may use body balancing techniques such as Qi Gong, Tai Chi, Yoga, massage or energy balancing. It includes meditation and soul-searching in all its forms.

While all of these methods are helpful to replenish inner reserves, these methods alone will not usually create self-love and self-acceptance. Noticing what you feel and then feeling it is still the key. These methods may help you begin to do that. When things get "out-of- synch", they will help bring you back to your center.

Loving yourself includes being a gracious receiver. Many of us have been taught that it is better to give than to receive. One cannot be better than the other because they are two aspects in the exchange of sharing. If it is better to give than to receive, can you really feel that fulfilled knowing that whoever you are giving to is inferior for receiving it? On the contrary, giving and receiving are two facets of wholeness. If you always give you will eventually become drained mentally, emotionally or physically. Receiving gladly and graciously completes the cycle. If you cannot do this you rob the giver of any joy they might have in being able to give to you.

Any hostility directed toward another is a symptom of emotional pain, lack of self-acceptance and lack of self-love. It is a crying out for acceptance. The irony is that while hostility indicates a need for self-acceptance, it is likely to push away that which we most hunger for. When we act out our hostility we damage our inner being. Guilt arises and then we act through our guilt as well. Someone who feels guilt cannot provide a high level of service to others. Guilt that is rationalized or vindicated by thoughts such as "he deserved it" is the most dangerous guilt because it does not allow recognition of the problem that lies within. It becomes a secret locked away in your heart for fear of being exposed. Forgive yourself for it. Find a way to make amends. When you recover your own well-being you will discover a world that is friendlier and more receptive to your presence.

The charismatic attraction of great spiritual leaders and world leaders who devoted their lives in service to the world is a result of their strong inner sense of self and the ability to forgive themselves and others. We are all capable of mistakes and errors in discernment. I use the word "discernment" rather than "judgment" here because it suggests a neutral clarity in making choices. It is more intuitive. I use the word "judgment" to describe preferences based on emotional reactions designed to make us feel better about ourselves but which have a destructive effect on our ability to carry on healthy loving relationships. If your ability to discern is clouded, it's because your heart is veiled with judgment. Acknowledge what you are feeling and what you have been hiding, then forgive yourself and make amends. The world is waiting for you.

For many, the task of forgiving themselves is so difficult. They have too many judgments to be able to do it. This is why people often turn to a religious icon. Through sincere repentance and the begging of forgiveness a new start is made. When the sense of self is so riddled by guilt and painful emotions, clearing the emotional body seems too overwhelming an obstacle. For them, surrender in this way is a path that provides healing. To work it must be more than lip-service - it must be a heartfelt and profound surrender. It is a mistake to assume that because it works well for some it is the only path. It is also a mistake to assume that just going to church or blindly accepting doctrine without an accompanying inner transformation will do anything to make the world a better place - or the one that follows for that matter. It is what is on the inside that counts.

Change within the heart and soul of individuals is what changes the world. The choice we make to heal ourselves is the choice to make the world a better place, by whatever path. Inner peace is a result of recognizing our eternal nature that is omniscient, omnipotent and omnipresent.

I was raised in a small, predominately Protestant Christian farming community and grew up going to church and Sunday school every week. Although I stopped going to church many years ago, today I hold the teachings of Jesus of Nazareth in higher regard than I ever did as an active member. I stopped going because I didn't see or feel the kind of inner peace I was searching for evident in the lives of those around me. I felt the teachings of this spiritual master had been squeezed into a simple formula, their profoundness mostly misunderstood or not grasped experientially at all. In my twenties I began expanding my viewpoint by exploring other avenues of spiritual training. I discovered a bigger picture. I began to see spiritual truth as many paths all leading to the same source, to The One. My understanding of the teachings of Jesus became broader, more far-reaching and all-encompassing. Spiritual truth is a personal journey we must each make for ourselves. My discernment has led me here but I will not judge who goes there. Only you know whether your heart is at peace or not. Only I can know for myself. All seek happiness. All seek the tranquility of a heart at peace.

When you are in tune with your soul purpose, life flows effortlessly without addiction to problem solving. Challenges may be met and overcome but the mind stops creating negative thought patterns that inhibit happiness and create resistance to whatever you are experiencing. A mind that is chattering away with self-talk about how stupid you are, how unworthy you are, how un-caring that person is, how selfish your partner is or how annoying a boss or co-worker is cannot effectively maintain the

intuitive soul connection that comes from higher self awareness necessary to calmly know your place in the world.
The way to accomplish this quiet understanding is by dealing with and healing every painful emotion as it occurs.
You must experience it to allow its passage. It's that simple.
Notice how it affects your body in a physical way. Explore
the richness and texture of it. Withhold any judgments
surrounding the feeling about yourself or others. Just feel.
At some point you will sense completeness, a feeling of
coming full circle, a satisfying feeling of release or simply a
fading away of the feeling.

Some people are unwilling to give up the drama
surrounding emotional experiences. They love the highs
and lows they think make them feel alive. It is important to
recognize that addiction to drama is a ploy to avoid feeling
what is really going on inside. It is a distraction from the
deeper pain that, if exposed, would make us feel even more
vulnerable than the dramas we are addicted to. Drama is
feeling with judgment that does not take responsibility for
one's life. It is feeling with blame attached. Addiction to
emotional drama will not lead to greater soul awareness
until the being tires of it. It may lead to a great deal of therapy in the meantime until the emotions are ready to run
clear. When they do, the light of Spirit can shine through the
person's experience.

Every painful feeling we've had, other than physical
pain, results from some sort of self-judgment. And I suspect
that even physical pain may be in on this more than most of
us are ready to believe. The conflict we feel with others, the
criticism we inflict, is a reflection of inner turmoil. It all
comes back to self. We must forgive ourselves for everything we don't like about ourselves, forgive ourselves for
feeling a certain way and forgive ourselves for inflicting
pain on others. But to truly forgive ourselves we must allow

ourselves the repentance that results from feeling the pain deeply. We make amends by dropping judgments about others in the future, and by recognizing that all judgments directed outward are reflections of an inner conflict. This must be experienced to be fully understood. Start by withholding self-judgment long enough to feel your pain. Forgive yourself. Then see the world through clearer, more compassionate eyes.

When a person who has been riddled with guilt, shame and covert intentions one day becomes completely overwhelmed and humiliated by the recognition of his "sinful nature", he may become a religious convert. Unable to forgive himself he begs forgiveness from God. Since he believes this is the only way to wash the soul clean, this actually works for him. Repentance is sincere. Many lives are changed this way but the self-empowerment, the embodiment of one's own divine nature, is displaced. Such people do not trust their own higher natures enough to feel guidance. Rather than find the peace that comes from an intuitive connection with one's creative nature arising from the source of higher self awareness, the person attempts to strengthen Spirit by associating with people who share the same beliefs and by trying to convince those who don't share their beliefs of the rightness of their path.

Nothing strengthens a being like forgiveness, but the most profound forgiveness is that which is directed toward the self, sincerely and with repentance. This is because after we learn to recognize ourselves in the faults we see in all the people we criticize and harbor grudges against, it becomes obvious that if we can forgive ourselves, everyone in our world will also be forgiven. A forgiving heart is a heart at peace with itself. Stop judging yourself. Acknowledge the part of yourself, the ego, that seeks to find comfort and glorify itself through manipulation and secret agendas.

Forgive yourself for it and make amends. Intend to do better. The less clouded your mind is with judgments, guilt and secrets the clearer your intention will be.

Self-worth is peace of mind under any circumstance. Accept yourself with all your faults and appreciate those faults as the unique manifestations of divinity they are. Then share yourself with the world by putting attention on others. Feel what they need. Offer your acceptance of them the way they are. In alleviating the suffering of others, suffering dissipates from your personal experience. The cycle of acceptance and regeneration continues. Through this path you will find peace, but first you must appreciate yourself as the worthy manifestation of divine power you are.

There is only wholeness. There is only One. There is no difference between you and me, the manifest and the unmanifest, the base and the divine. While incarnating in a body you experience yourself as separate from the whole. You are born on earth to remember your divinity. Divinity is the essence of who you are and is waiting for you to discover it. You were born to remember this. You know this. It doesn't matter how long it takes. The only hell you experience is the one you create by denying your spiritual nature. It is such a blessing to be able to go at your own pace. This is the gift of free will. There are no judges giving merit badges, only your own learning that contributes to the expansion of the collective soul. Enlightenment is contagious. You will find integration in your own time.

With trepidation
I walk the night;
Shadows flitting out
The corners of my eyes
Keen haunted cries.
I tremble.

15

Feelings

What exactly are feelings anyway? They are ephemeral in nature. The best way I know to describe them is as a welling up of charged energy within the medium of physical body experience. Feeling is pure. Feeling is the catalyst that transforms the raw material of experience into evolution for the soul. Emotion results when we make a decision in the form of a judgment about an event, circumstance or person (including ourselves). This usually causes the feeling to become stuck, so we continue to carry it around in our experience. By dropping the judgments that obscure pure feeling, one is able to let go of the limitations of the past. This path will lead home. Home is where love is. Home is where the Spirit of divine will resides within human form to create masterpieces of art in the expression of life. Love your feelings and you will begin to love all of life. Decisions that apply meanings to your feelings create a desire or resistance to the experience that is the cause of great suffering.

The shame we have as a society toward our feelings is reflected in many common phrases that describe our drive

to contain them. Here are some examples: "You must control your temper." "He swallowed his pride." "She bit her
lip to avoid saying what she felt." "He wore his heart on his
sleeve for the world to see." "She kept a lid on her anger."
"He was so excited he could hardly contain himself."
"He was fighting back the tears." "She was overjoyed."

Our soul longs for the experiential. That is its purpose
for being in a physical body. When we don't experience life
richly and rewardingly it is because we are blocking feelings. Feelings are the path to the mystical, the absolute.
I know many spiritual teachers have said that to achieve
enlightenment, or Nirvana, one must first transcend the
emotions. Like many other spiritual teachings, this idea is
nearly always misunderstood. Emotions can never be
transcended by an act of will alone, at least not with any
degree of permanence or stability. It is only by willingly
allowing the pure flow of feeling that you can experience
the peace of clear space beyond it. That is the way of
transcendence. That is the "dark night of the soul" that
every spiritual adept has passed through to attain wisdom
and peace.

By feeling the disowned parts of yourself, you are able
to feel greater compassion for others. You begin to judge
their shortcomings less and feel a greater sense of unity with
all others. "Others" become less "other" and more "us".

Feeling allows you to maintain your equilibrium in a
dynamic world, a world of constant change. By moving into
a feeling completely and experiencing all that it has to offer
you can experience the lightness that follows. Resisting a
feeling causes it to emanate a voice that nags from the
background of awareness. You find yourself unwillingly
re-playing scenarios over and over in your mind with no
resolution or satisfaction.

Observing yourself without judgment from a more unified field of awareness - your higher self - while simultaneously feeling all there is in the present moment is the intention of Spirit. Spirit desires to feel itself in an infinite variety of manifestations and the physical being longs to feel Spirit in its journey through life. The separation is maintained only by a free will that insists on continuing to judge. If you remove the judgments created by the mind there is only pure experience.

Free will is the gift of Spirit that gives your mind full creative rein. Whether you create primarily through the conscious, subconscious or super-conscious aspect of your mind, you continue to attract experiences based on the disposition of your individual outlook. This gift allows you to create and discern, to make choices about what and how you will experience. Your higher self, your godliness, exercises its free will to make choices that assist its evolution. This is the super-conscious, spiritual aspect of the mind.

The conscious mind intuitively communicates with Spirit but it also accumulates judgments based on conditioning and past experience that are stored subconsciously. As you move through life your mind, with its power to shape reality by belief and intention, becomes cloudy with judgments that obscure the purity of experience and separate it from Spirit. It creates new experiences based on the power and belief of those judgments. When this happens intuition fades and you feel separated from your divine nature. This is how free will continues to re-enact the fall from grace.

Feelings are the communication source from the spiritual to the physical body. They add richness to experience. They are the flavor of life. They only become unbearable when their richness and intensity is hampered by judgments from the mind. Emotions are feelings directed by judgments. Pure feeling is the experience of Spirit in the physical realm. It is the goal of Spirit and the essence of love. Rather than allow the mind to inhibit feeling and therefore Spirit, allow feeling to run its course. Feeling invites Spirit, which can always create something new for you to experience when you are ready to move on. Stop fearing your emotions. If you allow them they will lead you to re-discover yourself in expanded horizons.

Waking up to the spiritual sometimes comes as a sudden experience. It can occur during the mass excitement of a revival or in something as simple as noticing how a bug goes about its business. In such moments, all self-proclaimed identity is lost and the person is totally absorbed in the magnificence of the present. The experience of waking up is so dramatic, so life-changing, that it is usually difficult to let the moment go. You want to keep re-living the event. You cling to the memory, hoping to re-charge your spiritual batteries by continuing to re-experience it.

Experiencing an awakening is just the beginning of the real work. Clinging to the memory of it will drain you of the power that could be gained by continuing to exist in the present moment, whatever that is. An awakening is just that: an awakening. It is opening your eyes to previously unseen possibilities and getting a sense of the vastness of the divine that permeates all. It allows you to get a bigger picture and inspires you to transform your life.

The easiest way to get back to that state of grace is to begin experiencing what is in front of you right now. You must feel whatever is there. If you can let go of the judgments surrounding feelings and experiences long enough you will discover that you *are* the source of them. It is a humbling and amazing realization. It is a moment of spiritual expansion.

Remember to feel whatever is there, right now in the present moment. This is the shortest path to return to Spirit. Waking up to Spirit is remembering your true nature but you must remember to do it. Remember to feel here and now and you will remember who you are. *Eventually.* Event after event will remind you and *event*ually you will remember. You *are* the source of all you perceive. You *are* the source of your experience. You *are* one with God. It has never been otherwise. You have only forgotten.

The derivative of the word "Christ", according to Webster's New College Dictionary, is from the classic Greek word "chriein" meaning "to anoint." To be filled with Christ is to be anointed with Spirit. Christ is the light of Spirit that awakens in the hearts of humanity. Christ does not belong to a denomination or religion or a single person. Christ is a feeling. It is enlightenment. Christ is The One. Christ is the rapture and the bliss of feeling the Oneness. Christ is you *being* The One. Christ is communion with The One. Christ is all that is, including the emptiness of the Void out of which all that is arises.

Wisdom is the integration of knowledge and experience. We gain knowledge by taking in information and through instruction, but true wisdom is an inner knowing that is gained from experience. Children seldom learn through the advice of their elders because they are eager to have their own experiences. Relishing each moment as new and unique is the stuff of real wisdom.

The first step to wisdom is to allow the feelings we have held hostage in the form of emotions to flow within our beings. They seek freedom. They don't care about knowledge or understanding. They don't even care about judgments. Only the mind cares about judgments. Feelings seek only to move. The more mind lets go to allow feelings, the clearer our hearts become. The window to the soul is washed clean, allowing our higher natures to shine through. The gateway to our intuition opens. Life unfolds in fascinating fashion, guided by the wisdom of higher self.

Don't assume that because your emotions need release I am recommending you dump them out on someone else. The wisdom of the universe is within you, as is all the sorrow, happiness, pleasure or pain. I am inviting you to feel your emotions completely within the vastness of your being. Until now many of you have only been feeling the pain arising from self-righteousness and judgment. If you will let go of judgments long enough to access the underlying feelings they protect, the feelings can flow. It is not a painless process. But let's put it in perspective. Would you rather hurt a lot for a short time or feel a gnawing pain for the rest of your life?

Emotions held under control are already controlling the mind, which responds through further projection. The emotions take on a life of their own, becoming haunting voices that speak unbearable "truths" we fear about ourselves and our lives. They clamor inside our heads and give us no peace.

In allowing the feeling of and releasing your darkest aspects, you are doing a favor for all. Your thoughts and actions do affect everyone else in the collective mind. Thoughts create experience, which is a feeling event. If most of your feelings are negative and unpleasant, you are sending these thought forms out into the ethers of the universe to be experienced by all. And don't think that by hiding them from yourself you are doing anyone any favors, least of all yourself. They will only go unconscious. Your subconscious, which doesn't judge, will project them out into the world of your experience. The result is that you feel more and more out of control of your life. It is a paradox that to gain control of your life, you must first let go of controlling your feelings.

Thoughts and feelings are contagious. You have two options. You can spread good will by your harmonious intentions, which includes learning to feel your darkness, forgiving yourself for it and loving yourself anyway. Or you can contaminate the collective mind by the externalization of emotions, the expression of judgments and the projection onto others of your disowned darkness.

Your emotions held hostage poison the collective mind. Their darkness must be discovered and released by allowing the fullness of their experience within your feeling heart. You must own them completely, not give them away by blaming or attacking others. Only by owning them can they be neutralized.

The intention and willingness to embrace your own darkness will dissipate its power over you. You will be able to choose a new direction, one of a peaceful heart full of compassion, a direction that enhances your life and all those you know. Its ripples will flow out into the pool of the collective mind and you will be doing your part to transform global consciousness in a positive way. You will have helped bring the collective mind that much closer to remembrance of its divine nature, to remembering itself as The One.

Give me my sadness, my fear, my rage!
I won't leave that for someone else to clean up.
I will own what is mine;
Not pretend it's not there,
While trailing emotional debris.
You can change life by your thoughts,
But when you don't know the thoughts
Lurking in the caverns of your mind,
The shadowed recesses of your heart
Control you already.
They dwell, unloved, waiting to lash out
The moment you forget to re-affirm
That you are what they are not -
The moment someone pushes the right button.

16

Robotic Responses

Feelings are like the element of water. They are bubbling springs that need to rise to the surface of awareness. If held beneath the surface they may erupt like geysers, going off at intervals when a certain amount of pressure has been reached. A geyser may be more spectacular, but a bubbling spring is more nourishing. People stand back from a geyser in awe but a bubbling spring attracts them to its refreshing presence.

Many of us use those closest to us as sounding boards for the release of our emotions after our relationships have degenerated into robotic, button-pushing communications. It's important to really feel where the emotions are coming from. We must know what is going on inside us so we do not destroy the present by living through the filters of the past. Usually the other person is only a trigger for a latent emotion that already exists, not the cause of today's discord. In this case your beliefs and judgments have attracted a person who will "push your buttons" for you. His or her intention to do so may be purely subconscious - there may even be an agreement with you on a super-conscious level.

Before you were born you may have agreed to meet and challenge each other in specific ways. More than likely you are pushing the other person's buttons too, knowingly or unknowingly.

People often react to the actions of others in ways that don't feel good. They feel angry or hurt and respond in ways that perpetuate the painful experiences. Often their reactions are based on judgments formed as a result of past experiences that became personal truths, perpetuating the agony in present-time experience. Creating manipulations for power or reacting to them are both rooted in a feeling of powerlessness and a basic lack of connection to one's inherent self-worth.

The pattern continues until one of the persons changes his approach, changes his response or decides to create no response at all. Creating no response is not the same as bottling up a feeling. It is a recognition that you no longer need to be part of the other person's scenario. You are jumping off the merry-go-round. If you do not get back on, the other person will either jump off with you or find someone else to act out the drama with that will keep the merry-go-round spinning. Choosing to get off is a demonstration of the power of free will. It is choosing rather than reacting. Wouldn't you really rather choose experience than react to it?

Emotional responses are robotized reactions to stimuli that remind us of some early childhood experience or conditioning. The memory may be vague or even gone from conscious awareness but the stimuli triggers an automatic response based on an initial image in our memory. This initial image is our memory of the first encounter we had with something the subconscious mind considers emotionally powerful enough to store and similar enough to match it with what is happening now.

If our first experience of something is traumatic and we do not allow ourselves to fully engage it, the suppressed feeling is held in our subconscious mind and becomes part of our filter for future perceptions. Our reactions to all future experiences that evoke a similar feeling become ingrained in our consciousness, often without any awareness that it is happening. The reactions become conditioned responses and the way we respond to these situations is no longer current. It's like running an outdated program hardwired into your mental software. If an initial memory provokes a strong emotional reaction that is not fully embraced and released in the moment of its occurrence, this emotion continues to reassert itself whenever possible as the person matures, often continuing throughout a person's life if the experience is continually resisted.

Eventually we have a whole head full of mindsets that limit our pure experience in the present moment. This is why people often don't listen when you talk to them. They are unconsciously ruminating through all their stored judgments and memories, attempting to avoid facing an accumulating burden of toxic emotional baggage.

A common phrase in modern jargon is "getting your buttons pushed." This is what happens when a stimulus triggers an automatic emotional response. For example, pushing the robot button called rejection may cause some to feel depressed. Others react with anger or indifference. Anger may be masking a deep sadness and lack of self-esteem. Sadness could be masking a frustration with not being able or confident enough to express the anger felt at being rejected. Another person may feel a cool indifference at being rejected. The indifference may be masking a lack of self-esteem that it is protecting the person from knowing. We are all very creative about this. These automatic responses have no connection to the present. They are triggered by distant memories we are no longer consciously aware of.

As time goes on layers build upon layers until we no longer have any idea where feelings are coming from or why certain events trigger such strong emotions. Most people protect these layers and their inability to cope with them leads to a symbiotic and mutually dysfunctional relationship with another person, to an addictive behavior pattern or to some form of therapy. There is a difference between loving yourself enough to not let others' rejection of you affect your sense of self-worth and using indifference to bury feelings of worthlessness that really do exist. In the beginning of emotional recovery it can be difficult to know the difference. You must be meticulously honest to access the core of your feelings and re-awaken to Spirit.

Many of us are on remote control, responding to the agendas of our subconscious minds and buried emotions, which are operating from an old program. Our feeling software needs to be updated daily. This can only happen by bringing your experience of life into the present moment at all times. If you are living in the past, bring it into the present and get it over with, *now*. Your software will update as you move fully into the experience and allow it to dissipate of its own accord. Then you will be ready for something new.

Before you can re-program your life with new intentions, you must first erase the old recordings that play themselves out in your mind. Let your feelings be the guiding force. The mind then responds to the inner guidance. They are inextricably intertwined, but the mind cannot receive feelings, hunches and intuitions accurately when it is clouded by its own projections. If the conscious mind attempts to control feelings, they go "underground". Perverted by judgments they control the mind in a subconscious way, causing the mind to respond through further projection.

After this frustrating downward spiral has continued for a time (remember the cave paintings – a spiral can expand in either direction), our perceptions become so complex we are not even aware we are making judgments. We accept our perceptions, which we project onto the world, as indisputable fact. Operating through this convolution of beliefs attracts realities that continue to reinforce the beliefs. In order to get to a clear space we must recognize and deal with each judgment that obscures observation and pure feeling.

To experience a life unencumbered by the past you must first release the old charge by walking the dark narrow corridor of your repressed emotions. The end of the corridor is much closer than you may think. It only seems forbidding because you have not given yourself permission to go there. Our tears are the cleansers of our beings. They wash away the darkness.

"Walk in balance" is a common phrase today. I've noticed that for most people who use the phrase it seems to mean not experiencing anything too intensely. It is myopic to see any intense experience as a deviation from, rather than a return to, balance. Ask any saint or mystic who has attained inner peace. He or she will tell you that on the road to enlightenment, in addition to peak experiences of indescribable joy, there have also been bottomless abysses of the darkest, most dismal despair. The "dark night of the soul" grants passage to a clear and beautiful dawn. You cannot walk in balance until you know what it feels like to be off balance. Pretending doesn't work. You may fool others for a while but you will never fool yourself. It is a complete waste of energy that could be used to recover your inner power instead.

Here are a few ideas to help you get started in facilitating the integration of unwanted emotions. Take a few deep breaths, close your eyes and picture yourself in front of a very large mirror, a mirror of power. Think of a negative emotion you often feel or use one you are currently experiencing. Feel its essence. Let go of the judgments you have about feeling this way. After a few minutes of feeling it and with eyes still closed, imagine opening your eyes and looking into the mirror. What is the first impression you see? Use whatever you see as a starting point and describe it out loud into a personal tape recorder. Continue on for several minutes, describing the image. If it changes and evolves as you describe it, record that too. When you feel complete you may stop the meditation and listen to the recorded information or decide to let it "gestate" and listen to it a little later. Always use the first impression that comes to you as a starting point. It is a bit like dream analysis, but the images you are analyzing are those that emanate while you are in a waking, relaxed state. Allow your inner feelings to guide you as to the meaning for you. Images may be literal or metaphoric. This idea is an adaptation I use based on techniques for self-discovery found in a personal learning course called *Genius Code*, developed by Paul R. Scheele and Win Wenger and included in the references section at the back of this book.

Another exploration exercise is to sit quietly and think of a part of your body that has been giving you discomfort or disease. With your attention on that area of the body, allow yourself to feel whatever is there. Imagine all of your awareness inside that one area of your body. What does it feel like? Is there an emotion? Just feel it intensely for a while. After you have explored the area for a while, begin to wonder. If that part of you could speak for itself, what would it have to tell you? You may want to speak into a tape recorder as you did with the mirror meditation, or jot down insights as soon as you stop the exercise. The ideas and insights that occur while you are in a pure feeling mode are the ones that will be most helpful to you.

You will know you have integrated something useful when you feel better. Some integrations are gradual and subtle. Others may surface as major realizations that are off-the-chart in their euphoric and liberating nature. The joy of the process is the discovery of self. Once a discovery has been integrated a higher plateau of living is reached. If you keep rising high enough you will eventually reach a point of pure clear space. In this space there is endless possibility and you can begin to manifest a life that you truly desire. This is the realm of the higher self.

A third and powerful method of self-discovery and emotional integration is to journal your feelings. If you like to write, it can be very cathartic to express your feelings, uncensored, on paper or a computer screen. Once done you can burn or delete the writing in a ceremonial fashion. I like burning because it is an age-old symbol for transformation. If you use a computer you can print it out and then burn it, but you may want to delete it too. An alternative is to archive your journaling for perusal at a later time. I have occasionally read things I wrote to myself two or three, even twenty or thirty years later and been amazed at how differently I viewed the world when I wrote them. And sometimes I am struck by how something I wrote many years ago still feels relevant to me.

Whenever a strong feeling is triggered, go inside and follow the feeling. Get carried away with it in the privacy of your inner space. Notice and allow everything you feel. You may find it transforming into many other forms and containing many aspects, or it may just get more intense. Eventually, the intensity will subside and you may notice that the feeling is transformed or feels less connected to you. Notice the quietness within at such times. These are the times the inner voice of Spirit can most easily be heard.

Any time we deny ourselves the experience of a feeling, we're telling part of ourselves that it's not okay to exist. This reinforces the feeling many of us have that we're not acceptable as we are. You cannot have healthy self-esteem if you deny part of yourself the opportunity to exist. If you feel the opinions of others are essential to your self-esteem, you have given away your power to live life by your design. You must be here for yourself before you can be present for others. Once you have become present with your true inner nature, you will be able to be fully present for others.

Understanding mentally where feelings originate in the mental movie of your life can be interesting but it's not necessary and it's never enough. The important thing is to just allow a feeling to run its course without expectation. Sometimes this letting go will release an old charge that provides synchronistic life realizations and deep healing. But searching for an event, a point of origin, while in the midst of experiencing a strong feeling only hampers the recovery process. It is not always necessary to pinpoint a specific experience to be healed of troublesome emotion. Simply dropping judgments about the feelings and allowing them passage is often all that is necessary. Feel without expectation. Realizations will occur as they are appropriate.

Moving into the feeling of emotion rather than away from it opens the body to be more receptive of Spirit. As old charge is moved out Spirit fills the Void created. There is a magnetic attraction between Spirit and feelings of the heart. Understanding universal concepts and the synchronicity of it all is a magnificent feat of the mind, but is exactly why the mind is so capable of convincing us it can do everything. Don't leave the missing parts behind. Honor your feelings. Allow space in your life to fully experience them. Spirit moves in the body through the conduit of heartfelt feeling.

Anger is divine.
Grief is divine.
Joy is divine.
Love is divine.

Love is born of joy,
And joy is born of the wonder of life
In all its madness and order,
Embracing harmony out of chaos.
Only through its lack can we know what joy is.
My tears are the cleansers of my soul;
They wash clean the darkness.

It's no more degenerate to sink into pits of despair
Than to respect only those like ourselves,
Despising the ways of the rest.

Lovers of light hide behind mantras and ceremonies,
Gathering in groups to disown negativity and exalt their paths.
They flock to churches and temples
Finding shelter in self-righteous superiority,
Separated from the squalor of the planet.
They leave unloved anger behind;
It reflects back to them in the world's havoc.
But they do not see it,
They do not feel it,
Immunized as they are by the shot of judgment
That vaccinated them to prevent its experience.

Let the mad bull rage forth from his pen!
Let fear awaken me trembling!
Through it all, I feel the richness of life race through my being,
Evaporating as it is dissipated
Until a new feeling wells up like a geyser.
Euphoria lifts my spirit high,
Buoyant in the truth of collective soul.

17

Negative Emotions

You may wonder what purpose negative emotions could possibly serve. The answer is they are useful to the extent they alert you to the fact that you have lost connection to Spirit. The unpleasantness of hate, for example, is a wake-up call. It lets you know you have fallen from grace. You are away from Spirit and fragmented. Nobody's home. Hate fills the gap when some emotional need, arising from judgments, has been blocked. The paradox is that we need to experience feelings authentically to heal ourselves emotionally and to do that we must learn to appreciate the emotions we hate. You may hate your negative emotions but if you can find a way to appreciate them you'll find hatred disappearing from other areas of your personality as well. I'll go into this more in a bit.

Several basic emotions generally considered negative include fear, anger, sadness, greed and jealousy. Extremely unbalanced variations of these are terror, rage, grief and hate. Ultimately, fear is the source of all of these. Fear is the absolute opposite of love. Love is abundance and includes everything. Fear is scarcity and the absence of love.

Courage results from trust in the Universe and high self-esteem. Courage defends us from fear by its sense of purpose for the being it protects. Fear reflects our absence of trust. Behind any negative emotion there is a fear of loss: loss of love, loss of money, loss of face, loss of health, loss of self-respect or a combination of these. Because our emotions are laden with judgments they consume a huge portion of our attention in our attempts to control them. This causes them to become charged and magnetic in nature, drawing unwanted experiences to us.

Greed and envy emanate from a fear of not having enough. They are a result of judgments about scarcity in the universe. Greed and envy are exaggerated by a sense of disconnection from other human beings. When we don't recognize that we are all one global consciousness we don't realize that placing our self-interests ahead of another will have any negative rebounding effect. The feeling of lack is created by an absence of trust in the universe combined with a basic sense of unworthiness. Yet it is human nature to desire a state of abundance, which flows forth easily when love in present. Abundance is the essence of being fully present in the moment. It is not purely monetary. It consists of a sense of trust that all will work out well for you, including having personally fulfilling work, accessibility to solutions in problem-solving and enjoying satisfying relationships with other people as well as ease in having basic needs met and paying the bills. This sense of trust cannot exist when there is a basic feeling of unworthiness; the feeling of not being good enough will pervade everything you do.

A person who feels unworthy is either constantly trying to prove himself to someone whose approval he feels he needs, or is convinced that the only way to feel better about life is to manipulate others. Some attempt to overwork, over-achieve or over-produce in an attempt to prove worth. Some deal with a lack of self-worth by cheating, lying, being greedy or bullying. Yet others manipulate covertly, by constantly playing the role of victim. Their motives are veiled in an aura of self-righteousness or chronic sickness. They use their problems as tools to make others feel bad if they don't do what the victim wants. Most of us know someone like this. I don't mean to imply that those who are extremely ill are manipulators. Yet some do use their illness as a means to this end, even though the intention is often subconscious.

When we project our unworthiness into the world by being greedy or treating others unfairly, they will often reflect back our poor self-image by avoidance, hostility or dislike. The feeling of unworthiness becomes an endless loop that is continually played back. And yet even if those we treat poorly forgive us unconditionally, there is never enough external validation to heal the hole in a soul resulting from low self-esteem. Money won't do it. Awards, recognition or fame won't do it either. Neither will having lots of friends or a loving, supportive family. These may all help to facilitate a feeling of self-worth, but the effect is temporary unless we appreciate ourselves for the unique expressions of Spirit that we are. The validation of self-worth must come from within.

Each person has the task of learning to appreciate his or her presence in the world. This can only come about through self-knowledge realized in the experiential clarity of moments of pure feeling. When you know yourself in this way, you will also know others. You will feel an appreciation for who they are. You will sense the inter-connectedness between you and everything around you. The world will not feel separate from you. It is okay to have preferences about people and places. That's part of knowing your

path and finding your niche. But don't allow your preferences to get in the way of compassion. Anything you think,
feel or do that causes more feelings of separation causes
more disintegration in the fabric of society. Anything you
think, feel or do that increases compassion and a sense of
community is a move toward integration. Both have global
consequences.

Jealousy emanates from a fear of not being valued
enough. Jealousy is a fear of loss rooted in an insecurity that
requires love and self-esteem to be provided from a source
outside the self. It is a destructive emotion that compares
oneself unfavorably to others and arises from feelings of
inadequacy. Jealousy can only be overcome by making
peace with yourself and supporting yourself in being
who you truly are. Again, it is a matter of finding self-
esteem within your heart. If this is done, jealousy will no
longer arise as an issue in life. Feelings of jealousy alert us
to the fact that we are not complete and are looking for the
missing parts outside ourselves.

Anger often results when we do not feel in control of
our lives. People who live their lives as though they are
victims of circumstance feel powerless, frustrated and
angry. Their anger is covert and manipulative. Often when
basic assumptions about life or self are challenged, either by
others or by circumstances in our lives, the anger is more
blatant. The world becomes our punching bag. In both situations the anger is based on a fear of losing control, or of
having lost control, of our lives.

I spent the first thirty-five years or so of my life thinking I was not an angry person. In my twenties, when I began
exploring spiritual teachings that were different than what
I had always been taught, I thought of myself as a level-
headed, somewhat serious but deep thinker. I was very
mental about the whole idea of enlightenment, even though

I knew all the great spiritual teachings called for letting go of thought to achieve higher states of awareness. My inner nag chided me relentlessly for trying to figure everything out, but that didn't stop me from trying. Still I did not think of myself as having much anger.

You can imagine then, how amazed I was when one day a minor challenge to my ability to control my destiny caused me to recoil in agony, followed by an explosive demonstration of my anger. It was a challenge I had faced uneventfully many times before, but on this particular day it caused a torrent of latent rage to surge into my awareness.

At that time I created Southwestern-style fine art batiks that I sold at outdoor art and craft festivals all around the western portion of the United States. It involved a great deal of driving and setting up and tearing down of my display a couple of times a month. It was how I made a living. Applications for these festivals required "jurying", which meant sending several photographs or slides of my best work to the screening committees for each event. Due to a great deal of competition for the best shows, it was a fact of doing business this way that there were always many rejections. I had been going through a rough period financially. To try to adapt, I had changed my artistic style and subject matter. Even though I was still getting into most of the festivals I wanted to do, I was very insecure about my work and sales were still down. Since I considered the work an extension of my personality, it was hard not to take rejection personally, whether it came in the form of slow sales or not getting into the best venues.

One day, I received two rejection notices the same day for shows I considered important to my financial stability. To make matters worse I knew that most of my friends, who were also my peers, would be there. I would be missing important social events as well as opportunities to do well at some of the better festivals.

Frustration that had rumbled dormant while I endured months of slow sales finally got to me. At first I went to pieces. I locked myself in the bathroom and cried until my stomach tied itself in a knot. Then I remembered a fantasy I had often played out in my head at festivals when sales were slow. I would fantasize destroying pieces of my artwork. I decided to act out my fantasy now, because it was never acceptable to do it while I was sitting at my booth in public. There were always a few selections in my inventory that irritated me for whatever reason. Sometimes I just knew one would be a loser before I ever framed it but for lack of time or a need for a full display, the "loser" would make it into my collection of framed and finished pieces. I knew these were not my best work and when sales were slow, they added to my humiliation. I was embarrassed to show them and angry at myself for being stupid enough to think they could possibly work. It was time to end the feeling.

I went out to my workshop and ransacked my inventory, dragging out a couple I considered rejects. I took them outside. I smashed one of them onto the concrete parking area in front of the building. After months of carefully guarding them against damage while transporting them and setting up, I reveled in the sound of the glass breaking and delighted in scratching the metal frame against the concrete. I stomped on the back with my heavy winter boots.

I set up the other one in front of a stack of hay we had leaning against a storage building for feeding our horses and wild deer. I found the little twenty-two magnum derringer that Skip, my life partner, had insisted I buy to protect myself while I was on the road alone. I had never liked the idea of having a gun and after a year or so, had stopped bringing it on my road trips. But now I was glad I had it. I began to use the picture for target practice.

Each time the gun fired, my whole being reeled intensely with the discharge of energy and pent-up anger. It rolled out my extended arms toward my target and rocked me all the way down to my boots. As I riddled the painting with holes, older, less current anger surfaced. I was in an altered state and the world seemed surreal and distant. Things that had bothered me for years, things I had never fully gotten over, occurred to me and were released with explosive charge. My anger kept winding back until I was five years old and younger. Angry thoughts popped like firecrackers as I continued to fire away. Adrenalin surged through me and my whole body shook, yet I took remarkable aim. I paid no heed to the neighbors' dogs barking or to our horses running wild in the pasture. I shot until I was out of bullets, at least thirty or forty rounds.

Skip, who had been observing in quiet fascination, offered me his three fifty-seven magnum. I had never fired it before and was getting tired. It was even more deafening. After three shots of that, I felt drained, complete.

We went in the house and sat by the fire of our woodstove for about twenty minutes without saying a word. He opened a bottle of wine. We drank. Huge tears of sadness and relief rolled down my cheeks. We began to talk a little. I felt incoherent. All I could say was, "That was an incredible experience." He said, "Yes."

We went into the living room and turned on some rock music. We began to dance. The music felt exhilarating and I really got into the movement of the dance. My body and the music felt as one. I became euphoric, enchanted with the wonder of life and the mystery of emotion. I felt lighter than I had in many years. We were grinning at each other.

We danced until all we could do was sleep. I felt complete. Over thirty years of stored anger had been released in less than thirty minutes. The experience that triggered it had little to do with the anger that came out. As agonizing as it felt when it began, it transmuted to a peak experience that was an important part of my self-recovery.

Sadness is a fear of being alone in the world. At a deeper level it is a feeling of being disconnected from self. We know no one else can live our life for us. Our experiences, our points of view are our own, and we feel the consequences of our choices. If the choices result in a feeling of futility or purposelessness in life, sadness and depression follow. Grief, an extreme form of sadness, is often experienced after the death of a loved one, although this is certainly not the only way it manifests. Again, it is a reminder of how alone we are in the world.

At one time or another in our lives we all came up with a story about why we are the way we are. Our story is our ideas and beliefs about how the world operates in relation to us based on the composite of our experiences and our judgments about those experiences. It consists of ideas we have about ourselves prejudiced by our filtered perceptions. We can be very creative about making up our story. Unfortunately it prevents us from learning through current experience. It takes away the gratitude we would feel if we let go of our story and live spontaneously in full appreciation of the present moment. The story I used to tell myself was based on the idea that I had a reason to be sad, that no one loved me enough and I would always feel left out. Alone.

Here's how I justified my sad loneliness. My preschool years at Sunday church school had instilled a self-image of being sinful and unworthy. I was told to fear God and to love him. This just wasn't comfortable for me. I didn't know how to love someone or something I was afraid of. I felt unworthy and unsure. This lack of confidence did not benefit me at all when my self-esteem was later challenged by my first social experiences at school. By then my subconsciousness had brought on board the idea that I was a sinful and worthless wretch who needed to beg forgiveness to even be allowed to exist.

My Kindergarten class had ten children, with five girls and five boys. Most of us lived on farms near the tiny town the school was in. We sat at three tables, with all the girls except me at one table. I was assigned a table with the two meanest boys in the class, who would pinch my legs unmercifully under the table. I got sick that year with pneumonia. I was in the hospital and out of school for two weeks. My first year of socialization had been a disaster.

By first grade the other girls thought of me as an outsider and did not want to play with me. One of the girls assumed the position of "the boss" and no one challenged her. Every day at lunch she and the other girls sat on one side of the long lunch table and I had to sit either on the other side by the boys or on the end. Each day I would work up the courage to ask "the boss" what we were going to play after lunch at recess. I don't know why I continued to ask. Invariably her answer was "*You* can't play." One day I felt so hurt and frustrated that I came inside from recess and cried to my teacher about it. She had no idea how to deal with it so she told me, "Don't be a baby, just go outside and play with them!" I remember fighting back the tears as I went back outside and sat under the bleachers by the softball field, hoping no one would notice me. I felt alone and ashamed.

In first grade I also remember the boys teasing me at recess, calling me names like "Blimp", "Blob" and "Fat Legs". "The boss" told me her mother said I had baby fat. I thought I was going to die of humiliation! Being fat *and* a baby was just too much. I certainly couldn't cry about it or I would prove I really was a baby like my Kindergarten teacher had said. I just continued to hide my feelings. Although I was a bit chunky I was never really fat. But at this tender age these experiences instilled a chronic fear of obesity and a negative self-image about my body. I have obsessed about my weight much of my life and went on my first successful diet at age fourteen, losing about eighteen pounds. I believed no one would ever care for me unless I was thin.

The truth was I had not cared for myself for as long as I could remember. I did not think it was right to even consider wanting to. I had negative self-perceptions and I was sure others felt the same about me. As my life went on, no matter how nice someone was to me I usually felt certain they were hiding an underlying disgust. I felt sad to be who I was and ashamed of it at the same time.

Over thirty years later I began to let go of this feeling when I acknowledged that below the feelings of grief and sadness at my unworthiness, I *hated* those little kids in grade school and Kindergarten who teased and humiliated me, had hated them as long as I could remember knowing them. By not allowing myself to hate them I had hated myself instead, which caused me enormous grief. I needed to hate them thirty years later in order to move beyond the sadness that was permeating my life and to be able to begin to love myself. I didn't hate who they are now. I hated who they were then. Somewhere in the midst of feeling the hate, I felt a resurgence of respect for myself. Once I allowed myself this experience, the hatred gradually dissolved.

It completely lost its power. I felt compassion for all my tormentors. I recognized their need to act out was rooted in their own sense of unworthiness and powerlessness, which was reflecting my own back to me.

Another chapter from my "sad and lonely" story demonstrates how a resisted experience will continue to draw you to it until its feeling message is integrated. As an adult I made the decision not to have children of my own and had a sterilization operation at the age of twenty-four. I had convinced my first husband that if we wanted children later, we could adopt. Although that marriage ended within a year or so after my surgery, I later got married to a man who had joint custody of his four-year old girl. Eventually he ended up with full custody and although I did not want to be a step-mom, I found myself in that role. In retrospect she was an amazing, fun and adaptable child but my relationship with my husband was complicated by too much emotional baggage. Her birth mother remained in her life to a large degree which complicated matters even further.

After nearly four years we separated and I immediately fell in love with a newly divorced man with a five-year old daughter. I too was soon divorced and pursued the new love of my life, who I eventually came to know as my life partner, Skip. He and his ex-wife had joint custody of their daughter and her mom was still very much in her life – again. I didn't have as much in common with my new step-daughter as I had with the first one but the budding love between myself and this man was so overwhelming I thought all I had to do was try harder and everything would work out.

In both of these relationships with partners who had young daughters, the girls had enjoyed the exclusive adoration of their fathers until I came along. For myself, I had longed for an exclusive relationship with a man uncomplicated by the remnants of fallout from a past relationship, i.e. a child. Sensing the jealousy between daughters and myself, both fathers had become more inhibited in expressing love to either of us, a fact both daughters and I resented. In both situations the daughters and I felt alienated from each other and felt the other was causing alienation from the one man in both our lives. In each relationship the daughters became like clinging vines to their fathers. I reacted by choosing to feel like an outsider.

Sometime well into my second experience of step-motherhood, I realized I was feeling a gap with my own father. My negative feelings about my partner's relationship with his daughter - in both situations - had almost nothing to do with us and everything to do with my early relationship with my own dad. These feelings were triggered by my feeling that I had been an inadequate daughter. Watching my step-daughters with their dads drove the point home for me. I came from a family of five children and did not remember getting the abundance of attention that these girls received from their fathers. It didn't seem fair. I had grown up thinking of my dad as a hard worker who had a sense of humor but who could also be harsh and impatient. I had seen him lose his temper on numerous occasions and even though his anger was usually directed elsewhere — often it would be a cow, a horse or a piece of farm equipment he was working on – the threat of it frightened me. Growing up I did my best not to make waves. I let my insecurity about self get in the way.

The gap I felt with my own father was only my perception. I thought I had never felt as safe and protected around my dad as these daughters seemed to feel around their fathers. Their self-assuredness in their fathers' love had awakened feelings of grief and resentment over something I told myself I had missed. At the same time I realized my dad had always done the best he knew how and overall had been a terrific father. I knew that perhaps the fathers of my step-daughters were over-compensating for guilt they felt toward their daughters for ending the relationship with their mothers.

That chapter of my story ended when I was able to move into my sadness and sense of loss and really feel it. By running with the feeling I was able to see my father through new eyes. In the years after this I learned to love my father fearlessly and more deeply than I ever had before. Nothing had changed except my perception. I appreciated his gregarious nature, his ability to enjoy a full belly laugh, his curiosity and openness to new ideas and his ability to meet the challenge of raising five children on a farm in rural Iowa that was largely self-sufficient. Instead of grief I felt gratitude. Gratitude is what I feel to this day.

Hatred is a potpourri of our harshest judgments and most rejected feelings. In seeking the release that doesn't come these feelings compress and harden, distorting perceptions and twisting in upon themselves until they become menacing and unwholesome. Discover the message that hate has for you and you will get in touch with your deepest insecurities. By moving willingly into feelings of hate you have protectively hidden, you are put in touch with gapped areas of yourself that need attention. Hate is a poisonous emotion that reflects deeply buried judgments and feelings of vulnerability about self.

When I first discovered them and actually admitted to myself that I had them, it was extremely difficult to admit I had such feelings, even to myself. I could not discuss it with others. I was too ashamed. Later, when the feelings had run their course and lost much of their charge, I could tell others because I was no longer identified with the feelings. I felt detached from them. I was amazed at the extent to which emotions held hostage had tainted my perceptions in present time. Even more amazing was the transformational power of finally owning and then letting go of the deeply buried emotional charge. It was euphoric! I say this without shame, but not without humility. I describe them to inspire you to have the courage to face your own worst fears about feeling what lies within. Feelings are powerful teachers that can grant deep wisdom and infinite compassion. They are not who you are. They are what you experience. Experience is the great teacher.

Underlying all negative emotions is some form of fear. We fear not only death, sickness and accidental injury, we fear life itself, including success, happiness and the free expression of all our feelings. The hostility we may fear in others is a reflection of hostility we've repressed in ourselves but are afraid to look at. We're afraid of our anger and we think if we can keep it under control no one will know about it, including ourselves. Instead of getting in touch with our hostility most of us live in fear of the hostility we see in the world around us.

If fear is a sign of weakness, then fear of feeling fear is even weaker. You may fear that if you experience your unwanted feelings they will rule your life. The fact is, by not accepting them or even looking at them, they are ruling your life already. They continue to emerge in unwanted ways that do not benefit you or teach you anything except avoidance. They are inappropriate when they do emerge because they are tainted by judgments that inhibit their pure experience. The purpose of fear in a holistic sense is to serve the purpose of warning us of danger. It is a signal from the subconscious mind – an instinct – designed to preserve the body, allowing us to discover and fulfill our respective life missions. These missions are possibilities we set for ourselves before incarnating into a body. Fear must be counter-balanced by trust so that we are not foolishly trusting or blindly fearful. Blind fear is an all-encompassing fear that incapacitates the Spirit, including both a fear of death and a simultaneous fear of living life abundantly.

Fear of death brings up two emotional crisis points: fear of the unknown and the fear of not getting whatever life was supposed to offer. The unknown is usually feared to some degree whenever we push the limits of our self-defined comfort zones. The frightening thing about death is that aside from near-death experiences, we only get one chance in this particular incarnation to do it. We usually cannot turn it back. We know death of the physical body is inevitable, yet it contains unknowns. The other crisis point about death, a fear of not getting whatever life was supposed to offer, is the result of dying without living life purposefully and abundantly. It's like graduating from special training and realizing you don't know how to make the curriculum work for you, or that you did not understand the curriculum at all. Fear of not getting the point of life is a source of deep anxiety or frustration for many. It is often experienced at mid-life or as death appears closer as a result of illness, injury or old age.

Being free to experience your feelings will make your life richer than you ever thought possible. It may be uncomfortable at first because you are experiencing beyond the bounds of your familiar comfort zone. You are learning to open your heart. The heart is where love is but there are also angry hearts, broken hearts, sad hearts and fearful hearts. Just open your heart and let it all out. That is where the healing lies.

Without self-acceptance life will never feel truly happy and fulfilled. There will always be a lingering deep sadness, vague melancholy or rumbling anger. Recognizing that you love and forgive yourself without judgment or condemnation for the way you are ushers in grace. Loving yourself as you are in this moment provides a buffer of protection from the pains and trials of daily life. Please, give yourself the gift of grace by honoring your feelings.

Let us dive deep into the ocean of emotion
Discovering darkness untold.
What secrets lying buried at unspeakable depths?
What mysteries could your hidden caverns reveal?
An ocean of tears ebbs and flows,
Salt flavoring infinite lifetimes
With the sorrow of lives not yet complete,
Flavored by misunderstanding.

18

Karma, Forgiveness & Grace

Traditionally associated with spiritual doctrines of the Orient, the idea of karma is a subject that has received more attention in the West in the past few decades. The interest in Eastern forms of religion begun in the 1960's has expanded to make karma a household word that no longer carries an attachment to a religious group. The idea is similar to the Biblical teaching of "an eye for an eye, a tooth for a tooth."

Believing in karma is the modern way many cope with the seeming injustices in the world. We believe when a person does something we perceive as wrong, that his karma will ultimately provide justice. "What goes around comes around" is the modern catch-all phrase to express this. It is the politically correct way to say, "He will go to hell." Each person who looks honestly within knows that hell is nowhere to go. It's already here! At the same time, so is heaven.

Karma is the idea that when a person takes an action it has consequence in the world around him. All action begins with an intention. Intention has substance. If the intention is suppressed, its creative power is projected out into the world. The intender sees it in the world but does not acknowledge it within. He will see it acted out by someone who is in alignment with the intention. He has disowned it. He is offended by it and judgmental. Most of us do this. We say his karma will get him. In saying this we have disowned the negative karma of our own intentions. All karma is connected. Our collective mind is so intertwined that we cannot project evil and negativity into the world around us and continue to evolve as spiritual beings.

Each person must assume responsibility for the condition of the world by sincerely owning his or her personal contribution to it. This is a secret to releasing karma. It ushers in the state of grace. It is the gold that lies within, amidst the rubble and decay of lifetimes of destructive behavior patterns and thought forms. This is what happens when people who, in a moment of clarity, see the fullness and intensity of their own destructive karma, what has been called in Christianity their "sinful nature". The plea "God have mercy on me, a sinner!" is a moment of clarity and humility. By identifying completely with and taking responsibility for their own faults, secrets and manipulative intentions they see with great insight the degree to which they are connected to the world around them. In that moment of grace Spirit and mortal connect. Compassion for others is unconditional.

When someone owns his own karma in this manner, it is a turning point. The soul has awakened within the person. Aware of his contribution to the state of the world, the person is genuinely humbled and feels compassion for all those around. There is a desire to help, to serve Spirit in a way that helps others relieve their own suffering. Being able to feel compassion for those still living in darkness is a good start, but most who have awakened will want to do more. Often, people who have experienced such a radical awakening become evangelists of their insights. I use "evangelize" in its broadest sense, because this tendency is not limited only to conservative Christians. If the awakened person develops a superior or righteous attitude, he or she will lack real compassion and increase the feeling of separation from others. Feeling grateful toward everyone you come in contact with for the unique presence they bring and for what they can show you about yourself will do a great deal more to change the collective mind than a world of evangelizing.

The fact that you have awakened from your spiritual slumber does not mean you will be free from karma. The awakening is the beginning of the real Spirit work. When you can easily feel yourself in others in any given situation, the "doing" of life will have become a holy act in and of itself. That is the glory of The One. That is The One incarnate. That is what we, in the image of The One, are here to do. We are here to experience The One while in a physical body, to know heaven on earth. Ignorance of this principle creates hell on earth. Heaven and hell are right here at all times. Hell is what we usually experience by feeling separate from other creatures and hence our divine natures.

Any time you feel hostility, superiority, inferiority or any other unbalanced emotion toward another person, ask yourself, "What have I not forgiven myself for?" Get very quiet and still and continue to ask yourself. At first nothing may come. Eventually, if you persist, a realization or connection of some kind will float to the surface of your awareness. It may not have anything to do with the thing you feel toward the other person in a rational sense. It is only that the other person triggers something inside you.

As an example, for years I have had a successful career in real estate sales. At one point several years ago I found myself feeling anger and hostility toward an agent from another office I was working with on the same transaction. I was working with the buyer and she was working with the seller. It was one of those rare but easy transactions that should have been a simple "slam dunk", as we sometimes called it in the business. The other agent seemed to be doing everything she could to complicate it. Whenever we spoke her tone was contrary, self-righteous and condescending. I had always considered myself easy to work with but she didn't seem to want or know how to let it be easy. She aroused my ire in a way I had not experienced working with any other agent. I would dread having to call her about some detail. She was impossible!

At first I tried to feel compassion, knowing how painful it must be to be inside her head, but soon I had lost my calm center and was becoming more and more irritated. When it was beginning to get the best of me, I examined this by asking myself persistently, "What have I not forgiven myself for?" I realized it was the idea that I was not perfect. Her "in your face" way of challenging everything I said or did and making a simple deal complicated and tense not only angered me, I found it impossible to respond to her in a way that seemed satisfying to her or had any resolution for me. I was very frustrated. I had always thought of myself as an excellent communicator. Here she was, making me feel as if I could not communicate at all! She wouldn't listen to me and yet she wouldn't stop talking either. Whew!

When I realized she was mirroring my fear that I'm not perfect, I knew I had found the source of my frustration. I thought, "Oh that! Yes indeed, I do set high standards for myself and can be quite unforgiving of results that do not meet my ideal. Okay, I'm not perfect – yet. But I'll keep trying." My higher self smiled in detached observation, knowing that I am perfect in my imperfection. The imperfection is part of an overall perfect plan!

With this understanding integrated I was able to actually feel genuine compassion for her. She too is seeking happiness and is doing her best to have it with what she knows. Her feelings and judgments may be frozen in some remote region of glacial tundra, but sometime, any day, the sun will become warmer, the weather will change and the softness of her soul will emerge like an infant with eyes wide open at the fascination of existence.

The world is your mirror. It doesn't mean the reflection you are seeing is exactly what you are being, but it is definitely a reflection of your perceptions and judgments. For example, you may see someone as arrogant. The mirror may be one of your own resisted arrogance. It could also be a fear that you dare not assert your opinions in front of others – the underlying judgment could be that you are unworthy of being heard, will be criticized or seen as arrogant yourself. Perhaps the arrogance you see in others mirrors a feeling of powerlessness in yourself that you don't usually notice but find disturbing when triggered. There are an infinite number of takes on this and each would depend on the beliefs and judgments held by the perceiver. The more you see a particular kind of reflection in your daily life, the more you need to feel what it is showing you about yourself.

A good way to explore the power of forgiveness in your life is to make it a daily exercise. Think of any unbalanced emotion you might be feeling toward another person. State out loud that you forgive so-and-so for whatever. Then ask yourself, "What have I not forgiven myself for?" Do this for as many things as you can think of. If that seems overwhelming, then start by spending ten minutes a day doing this.

It is good to give a concrete form to the forgiveness exercise. Writing them down first is helpful. You may discover feelings you had not thought about or acknowledged for years. You will probably be amazed, as I was, at how many things start popping up. You may even have dreams that include people you still need to consider forgiving. That is just your subconscious at work, bringing your attention to matters that have been obscured for a long time. You can follow this exercise by writing out declarations that express your willingness to accept yourself and others as they are.

When I started doing this, I forgave everything that came up, real or imagined. I forgave my mother for making me clean my dinner plate. I forgave the boys in my first grade class for teasing me and calling me "Blob" and "Fat Legs". I forgave my grade school classmates for intentionally leaving me out of their activities. I forgave my high school girlfriends for cruelly and unexpectedly turning their backs on my friendship. I forgave my college boyfriend for breaking up with me. I forgave my first husband for wanting children when I didn't. I forgave my second husband for not being ashamed to take help from his parents when we needed it. I forgave, I forgave and then I forgave some more.

Examining the resentments I carried that I thought needed forgiveness was like opening the proverbial Pandora's Box. Once I opened the lid, a lot of stuff came out. There was a lot in there to look at! It was really quite fascinating. I just kept doing new forgivenesses as newly recognized resentments popped up. Sometimes old ones kept re-surfacing. I just kept exploring every aspect of the resentment and forgiving whoever or whatever came up to blame. I realized that I had been placing so much attention on my criticisms and resentments that I had little or no

attention span with which to focus on what I might actually want to create in my life. I discovered that the more I forgave, the more ideas I could conceive for wonderful new
possibilities in my life.

Many times the forgiving will not be for actual wrongdoings but for your *perceptions* of wrongdoings. For example, I forgave my younger sister for getting more of my
father's attention and love when we were small girls. It was
not that he actually loved her more or gave her more attention or that she had ever done anything to make me feel
less. She was who she was. It was my idea about her that
I needed to forgive. My mistake was in comparing myself to
someone else. In retrospect, I realize my father was a master
at loving all of his children in individual ways. He appreciated the diversity and uniqueness in each of his five
children and his relationship to each was uniquely special.

At one point I even had to forgive my wonderful life
partner, Skip, for being more successful than I was, because
at that time I was struggling financially. Then I had to forgive myself for needing to forgive him for being successful!
Until I could really forgive him, there was no room for
success in my own life.

I forgave all the friends I have had in my life for
anything they had ever done that bothered me and for new
things that came up *as* they bothered me. Using the mirror
concept, I also forgave myself for qualities I saw as needing
forgiveness in others. I found much that needed forgiving in
myself, including the fact that I demanded perfection and
wasn't perfect.

Forgiveness serves the purpose of releasing the baggage of judgment so you can come back into present time
with your feelings. Forgiveness is the corollary, the shadow
side, of a declaration or affirmation. When something you

are intending is not resulting in a manifestation of what you would like to receive in your life, there is an opportunity to forgive that needs to be recognized. Forgiving self or another frees up the necessary attention for your mind to be able to create something different. A reality cluttered by resentments inhibits creative power because there is not enough free space in your sphere of intention with which to create what is desired. In computer-speak, your RAM (random access memory) is full! It is completely wrapped up in trying to cope with or resist circumstances you do not believe you are the source of. Lack of forgiveness renders one powerless.

Find a way to make forgiveness real in whatever way works for you. It is not necessary to inform the person you are forgiving of what you are doing. In fact, it may be better not to in most cases. Many times the person you are forgiving has no idea how you feel because your pain is often a fabrication created from judgments emanating in your mind. You are doing this for yourself. Here are some ideas to access the lifeline that forgiveness offers:

Write a forgiveness statement ten times on a piece of paper. Say the words aloud as you write them if you are alone. Then re-read the words aloud and dispose of the paper in whatever way feels appropriate. You can burn it, shred it, wad it up and throw it in the trash, whatever.

If you like to look back later over writing that reminds you of how far you have come, you might do the previous exercise but instead of disposing of the paper, place it in a special file in a filing cabinet, labeled "The Forgiven".

If you like ceremony you can make disposing of your forgiveness papers a ritual. Set up an area with candles, incense, religious icons or whatever makes you feel good. Release your forgivenesses to the universe and visualize them being wafted away and neutralized. You can vary this any way that suits you. Perhaps you would rather do it outside next to a large old tree and visualize the forgivenesses being absorbed by the tree and sent deep into the earth for purification. Make it meaningful for *you*.

You may prefer to tell your forgivenesses to a spiritual teacher or leader, saint or role model that has power for you. That being does not necessarily need to be present in physical form although it could be.

Declare and release your forgivenesses to the universe. The more feeling you can put into this the better. Try saying them out loud with arms held upward and outstretched in a gesture of letting go. Or, if it feels more appropriate, fall down on your knees, bow your head and whisper your forgiveness. Feeling them is important, as it opens the conduit to Spirit.

Before you can transform your negative emotions you must forgive yourself for having them. Forgiveness is the key to accepting our darkness with all of our negativity and all of our unwanted feelings. It is a necessary step toward genuine spiritual awakening.

At one point in my life I was intensely examining my own judgments. I was struggling in an effort to let them go. It was three o'clock in the morning and unable to sleep, I had been sitting out on my front porch listening to the distant surf of the Gulf of Mexico, pondering the chaos and confusion in my mind. A most amazing revelation suddenly occurred. I finally got that all the criticisms, anger, hostility and aloofness I felt toward others - and yet tried to keep internal - were just reflections of my unforgiven shortcomings. I was stunned. Although I was alone I actually felt embarrassed to be in my own presence! It was one of the most humbling experiences of my life. I was in awe at the realization - it completely blew my mind. "Could it really be that I am judging myself that much?" I wondered. "Could it really be that all of the people and situations I feel critical of in my life are just external projections of my internal self-condemnation?" I began to realize I had been an emotional mess most of my life but until then I did not have a clue. My mind had been too busy being a "spiritual seeker", all the while attempting to contain a potpourri of hostile judgments about myself projected onto people around me. I felt shamed before myself. I began to sob. The feelings ran deep. I felt raw, exposed and extremely vulnerable. In the distance I thought I heard a whale calling.

My bleeding heart was going through a remarkable transformation. It emerged later that day as if sprung from a trap. I experienced an incredible sense of euphoria, inner strength and presence in the moment. As the days passed, my euphoria floated back down to a more ordinary state of being but I haven't been the same since. It was a very healing experience.

This doesn't mean I never fell to another low. However, all subsequent lows have drifted through my life on the wisdom of this new understanding, allowing me to be more spiritually prepared to deal with them. Spirit takes us many places on our journey through life. By judging less I have found life to be more fascinating and less painfully challenging.

Humility is the usher of compassion. It causes us to realize that we are no less and no more than others in the world around us. We are all One. We are The One. My lowest lows have always been accompanied by some form of self-judgment or criticism. Lows that are felt rather than continually resisted by judgments transform the pain of humiliation into the power of humility.

Humility cares without judging. It does not see inferior or superior. It sees a larger picture. Humility does not degrade but sees oneness in the magnitude. Humility feels compassion. Humility allows the richness of life. It is not self-effacing, nor is it pitiful or powerless. It is not a martyr. In fact, feeling genuine humility is a way of awakening to spiritual power. It is the dawn of enlightenment.

Ripples roll out of creation through the silence of space,
Their movement a vibration, a distant clamor
Echoing into emptiness, absorbed by the silence of The One,
That which hears all in quiet fascination.

19

The Infinite Loop of Silence and Vibration

Silence is a retreat from the outer world and yet it contains everything. The creation of something starts with a vibration. All vibration has a sound, even the vibration of intention. Some sounds are not perceptible to human ears. When you become silent for a while, sounds that are not perceived in the cacophony of daily life emerge into conscious awareness. If you focus on a particular sound and follow this awareness to its source, silence occurs. It is not that the vibration has stopped. It's just that conscious awareness of the sound as something separate from yourself has ceased. You have entered the Void, or "the emptiness" of Qi Gong. In this pure state, silence and sound are no different.

The emanation of creation out of vibration was described this way in the Biblical book of Genesis. "In the beginning was the Word, and the Word was with God and the Word WAS God." God was described as the essence of the vibration out of which all manifestation springs. Silence is a return to the source of vibration, the limitless unmanifest.

Both silence and vibration are aspects of The One. They represent the dualistic way of thinking we seem to find necessary to describe the physical universe. You cannot have one without the other because awareness of one creates awareness of its opposite. Other examples of this are concepts which require an opposite to be understood such as good/evil, in/out, male/female, up/down, hot/cold, dark/light, etc. This is the essence of Yin/Yang theory in Eastern mysticism, which describes in a similar way the dualistic nature of the physical universe experience.

As we evolve through existence our vibrations increase in frequency. The frequency begins to be perceived on another level, becoming less audible on the mundane level. A person becomes more in touch with his own creative ability as the frequency increases. Life transforms into a symphony in which he finds himself the director. He may seem mostly the same to those around him, but his own perception is different. He is experiencing life from a different level of vibration.

The highest vibrations have the most creative power. They are moving so fast they appear not to move. Eventually they merge as One. The One contains all creation and yet, is perceived by aspects of itself vibrating at a lower level to be not vibrating at all. This is the Silence that contains unlimited potential. Because there is no resistance, nothing further is created.

In order to create, a new vibration must originate from the emptiness of Silence. In order for it to move it must resist something. Desire and resistance to what is create the endless loop of infinity. Desire is a resistance to not having something and resistance is a desire to not have something. They are really no different in their ability to attract circumstances to our lives. Too much of either creates a life of hell. This is the wheel of suffering described in the Eastern Vedic texts. There is an old saying that what you resist persists. I find it very useful to keep this in mind.

Meditation is a practice that by its nature withdraws attention from the desires and resistances that normally occupy a large portion of our thought processes. In this state of undisturbed calm the mind is receptive to the voice of Spirit. Intuitive ability is increased by meditation because it allows the voice of higher self to be heard. When the mind is clamoring with judgments, rationalizations, desires, resistances and obsessions, the voice of Spirit is difficult, if not impossible, to hear.

Messages from Spirit are transmitted through super-conscious awareness via hunches, insights, "gut feelings" and visual imagery. Rational thinking obscures their perception. This is why meditation is often taught by having the pupil focus attention on a mantra. The word has no logical meaning to the meditator. The idea is to focus attention on something that does not bring up distracting thoughts, lulling the mind into a quiet, receptive state and ultimately, enlightenment. For many, meditation has become a lifetime habit and daily devotion, reducing stress and bringing greater clarity. Others find it boring or feel they cannot focus their attention well enough to produce a worthwhile result, declaring it is a waste of valuable time.

I have found there are other ways to experience the benefits of meditation that are both enjoyable and more entertaining. Attention becomes fascinated and focused, making it easy to slip into a state of quiet receptivity without the conscious mind noticing.

Have you ever sat and just gazed at the lines on a rock? Really examined them? Or perhaps stared with wonder into the complexity of a flower's center? Have you stopped to notice the pattern of mold on a tree or the structure of its bark? As children most of us found fascination in close examination of the world around us. It's a very calming and empowering, albeit subtle, activity. Unfortunately many of us stop taking time for it as we grow older. We get caught up in the duties of our day and forget about the importance it once had in our lives when we had nothing "better" to do. It is quite literally an exercise in taking time to "stop and smell the roses". Although objects in nature are rich with detail and feel intrinsically soothing when observed this way, fascination with anything will work: a painting, the craftsmanship of a table, anything that is right in front of you.

Taking the time to quietly observe the details of something leads to a contemplative state of mind that is like meditation. You may find it an easier way to quiet your mind than more formal meditation practices.

Listening to music that makes you feel good can be used this way too. Sometimes even loud music can have this effect if the listener is involved enough. Witness the loud music of tribal rhythms, designed to induce altered states of consciousness. I used to attend a weekly workshop where one of the exercises was for participants to lie on the floor while listening to a thirty-minute musical selection played at a very loud volume. The purpose was to induce waking dream-like images in an altered state. I've had the same effect doing this on my own by listening to everything ranging from the sounds of Tibetan bells to intense rock music.

Communing with a pet in silent togetherness is another great method of contemplation. Pets are very telepathic and are usually quietly receptive to this kind of attention. Don't expect a particular kind of response from your pets, just observe and appreciate them as they are.

When we contemplate something a while, we may slip into a state of passive awareness. From there it is a short jump to the Void, the silent space within where the world of matter ceases to exist.

This quiet space within hears nothing of the outside world. It hums along in the background independent of even the still small voice within your heart that guides your life. In this pregnant, yet vacant space it appears even to the one experiencing it that nothing at all is being experienced. There seems to be no awareness. It is a state of non-manifestation. This non-reality is the groundless being-ness from which the creative production of all experience emerges.

For free will to be effective, one must first drift into this ethereal nothingness where the mind at last finds rest. The fewer things the mind is dwelling on, the easier access to this realm becomes. When creative attention is already fixed on the manifestations currently existing in one's life, change is difficult or impossible.

The vacuum of non-experience attracts its opposite, a desire to manifest a something. These creations are ordinarily experienced through the filters of past creations of experience. When we have let go of enough judgments to be able to live more fully in the present, we arrive at a point where experience is fresh and less hindered by the past, and there is less concern about the future. When past experiences are remembered without judgment they are now part of the present – they no longer keep us stuck in the past. The future is an intention that exists now, and that intention, whether based on fear or love, also determines the quality of the present.

The present is pre-sent. Our experience of the present is an intention delivered to the cosmos that announces our state of being at any given moment. This combination of feelings and judgments is like a radio that sends out a frequency. The frequency is picked up by possibilities that exist in the realm of unlimited potential that are attracted to it. These possibilities arrange themselves in interesting and unique ways within the environment and mind of the person sending the signals. Through the power of choice and the filter of whatever perceptions are present, the moment of now continues to unfold in alignment with our deepest nature. The moment of now is always a new moment.

There is another way to induce the benefits of meditation without actually sitting down to meditate. That is to become so fascinated with whatever you are feeling or experiencing, with whatever is right in front of you at all times, that judgments and rationalizations fall away. Mental concepts give way to the feeling of the moment. The heart becomes a conduit for intuitions and realizations from the higher self. Life becomes an active meditation and the world becomes a temple. Intuition becomes the spiritual leader, guiding you through experience while keeping you connected to the sacred.

Make each moment so important that it is worth your full attention. Be fascinated with what is right in front of you, with what is already inside you, and your life will take on a whole new flavor. There is nothing to seek "out there".

Love of life is the nature of spiritual experience. Any form of fear is a lack of love and therefore a lack of spiritual feeling. You must walk through your fears to get to the love. Whatever you fear most is your biggest challenge. Facing the fear provides the potential for your greatest reward. The reward is being in a state of love, the multi-faceted jewel that reflects peace, wisdom, bliss, grace, oneness, self-knowledge, ecstasy, compassion, amazement, purposefulness, empathy, fascination and joy in your life. It is the Holy Grail, the prize of existence. Your entire purpose is to discover your love and thus, your divine nature. The embodiment of its multifaceted aspects raises the consciousness of the planet.

"If you take this advanced formula it will change
your body chemistry

And you may begin to feel better, at least for a while,"
the doctor invited.

"But it may be more effective to change your mind.

This too can change your body chemistry

And may cause you to feel better with no side effects."

20

Body Chemistry and Emotions

Although intention rules the results we see in our lives, this discussion would not be complete without addressing the effects various substances have on our body chemistries that in turn affect our emotions. After all, one aspect of our experience is physical. Although I am not a nutritionist or medical doctor, I have been an avid free-lance student of holistic health and wellness for nearly thirty years. During this time I've taken notice of how certain foods and substances affect me, and I've watched the Western attitudes about what constitutes health change dramatically over the years. I believe this short chapter is worth considering for its possible value in facilitating the release of toxic emotions. It is not a cop-out for taking responsibility for your life as it is now. Instead it should serve as one more tool to assist you in securing the life you want and deserve.

Hormones of all kinds are chemicals that can radically affect our emotional outlook but we have somewhat less control over these than substances we take intentionally. The best advice I can give is to become informed about nutritional supplementation so these natural body chemicals stay in balance as much as possible.

Environmental toxins overload the liver. This includes substances such as exhaust fumes, pest sprays and chemicals in processed foods, as well as things we take in our bodies intentionally, including pharmaceutical drugs, caffeine, alcohol and skin care products. Chemicals and drugs absorbed through the skin can be just as toxic as those that are swallowed or inhaled.

In Chinese medicine theory the liver is considered a repository for anger held in the body. When the liver becomes overburdened with chemicals, anger often arises spontaneously and habitually. Consider the increasing concern over road rage in recent years.

Caffeine, sugar, alcohol and drugs have been shown over and over again to alter the chemistry of our bodies in ways that are not only unhealthy, but that trigger unwanted emotional reactions. They inhibit in the sense that they block true feelings and create new ones that are artificially induced. The letdown from eating sweets is commonly known to produce "sugar blues".

Caffeine and sugar both set up cravings for more and some people seem more susceptible to this than others. For some they are as addictive as alcohol is for the alcoholic. These are the people most likely to be affected in a negative way emotionally by the very substances they crave.

For over fifteen years I was a caffeine maniac, drinking coffee all day long and usually a few colas too. When I decided to quit using caffeine I went through an intense withdrawal with a stubbornly persistent headache that lasted for several days. During that time I was groggy and disoriented. My thinking was very unclear. During the weeks that followed I would occasionally test to see if

I could have a cup of "real" coffee (not decaffeinated) or a few caffeinated sodas without any ill effects.

What I began to notice was that every time I had two or three caffeinated beverages within one day, I would be sure to have an episode of feeling completely irritated with the world and everyone in it forty-eight hours later. It was like clockwork and when it hit, I felt I had no control over the feelings. Eventually I learned that the best thing to do was to just hide for a while until the feeling passed so I did not offend anyone, although I have to say, when the mood hit me, I really didn't care. The time delay between ingestion and irritation was so long it took me many months of repeatedly isolating a period of caffeine ingestion and then noticing the mood swing forty-eight hours later after having no caffeine to realize what was happening.

After a while I realized I could even notice the effect of one cola or coffee in forty-eight hours. It happened every time without fail. The irritability would always sneak up on me and catch me off guard. I wouldn't realize what was happening until I was right in the middle of a bad mood. The caffeine had its own repertoire of attitudes and negative self-talk that was specific to its usage. It was almost like playing a tape because the responses it evoked in my mind were so predictable. I would find myself snapping at my partner or feeling totally impatient with my life for no apparent reason. In my head I would be packed up, out the door and moved to another state as the destructive self-talk continued. Then it would dawn on me: "It's the diet cola I had two days ago" or something similar. Usually even after I realized the cause I would not want to or would feel unable to change my mood. I just had to ride it out.

In all my years of heavy coffee drinking I was under the illusion that I was not a morning person. I could hardly say two civil words to anyone before I'd finished at least one cup of coffee in the morning. I just thought I had a bad morning personality! Although caffeine was difficult for me to give up it was a relief. Without its influence I was not only more pleasant to be around but felt more content in general. I became able to keep my energy at a more even level throughout the day. I discovered I could get through the day even better without it.

If you want to be in touch with your true feelings and not create episodes of emotional outburst that have almost nothing to do with what is happening in present time, you should monitor your intake of caffeine, sugar, alcohol and drugs of all kinds, prescription or otherwise. You may find that many of your emotions are coming from a coffee cup!

Any foods that you eat a lot of or crave are also suspect, as your body may have developed food sensitivities to these things. Common items that are known to cause food sensitivities are wheat, rice, soy, corn and dairy products. Keep a mood-monitoring chart or calendar where you note days and times you used one of these substances and also keep track of periods of intense emotional feeling, particularly those that seem to have no cause. Some effects may be immediate, while others may take a couple of days to manifest symptoms. You should also note any physical reactions, such as sudden fatigue, rashes, eczema, buzzing feelings on your body or face, etc. There is an abundance of information online and in books sold in health food stores as well as conventional bookstores if you would like more information about food sensitivities and food allergies.

If you are taking prescription drugs that cannot be changed or reduced, at least become aware of the influence. We all have unique chemistries and some of us respond more or less to a particular substance. When tranquilizers and pain killers are wearing off, they can plummet a person to the pits of black depression and despair. Amphetamines and cocaine make the user high-strung and impatient, as do many prescription drugs. Most drugs will eventually fill the mind of the person using them with paranoia, irritability or both.

Alcohol and marijuana tend to dull the senses to the point where emotions don't seem to matter any more, although people react differently. For some, alcohol causes them to become more emotional or to become violent and verbally abusive. I'm not saying you should never have a candy bar, a cocktail or your favorite coffee beverage. But practice moderation and begin to monitor the effect these substances have on you. You may gradually find yourself wanting to change or stop your intake of these substances.

Prayer of the Shaman

Chant the sacred chants;
Dance the sacred dance;
Heal me,
Feel me,
Set me free.
Go my spirit to ride the night;
Help me emerge into the light;
I must find a way out of this plight.
Chant the dance;
Dance the chants.
Heal…
Feel…
Set free…
I am me.

21

Soul Fragments

Judgments are the ultimate separator. They separate us from each other, from ourselves and from The One. Our judgments about a particular situation keep us from allowing the intensity of feeling that would have us fully experience it. By not fully experiencing it we become a collection of fragments of disowned and dismissed – but not discarded – emotions. They attach themselves to our psyche by our resistance to them. We become crippled by our emotional baggage, unable to fully enjoy life.

When these fragments build up enough, we may find we no longer feel much of anything anymore. Numbness prevails and the joy of living has disappeared into the shadows. We no longer know who we are.

When you dive into a deep pool of emotion and feel you might drown remember, "This too shall pass." A feeling that is not allowed or even acknowledged will literally come back to haunt you again and again. It will take on a life of its own because of your separation from it, until you are absolutely convinced that it is not yours at all. It will continue to torment you in twisted and disguised ways. Whatever it can do to try to reach you it will do.

Common side effects of disowned emotions over a long period are an underlying sadness or anger or both, feeling like a victim, addictions, anti-social behavior and physical illness, particularly chronic illness. Some physical illnesses and limitations are willingly experienced with an attitude of surrender by the persons having them as life lessons leading home to higher self, which they can be. For others the illness is a condensation of damaging emotional energy that finds its only release in the physical illness of the body it inhabits.

The world is our mirror. Our perceptions reflect back to us the thoughts, fears and expectations we hold present most consistently throughout our experience. When we make a judgment about someone we create an expectation for the future and tend to see that person through the filter of our judgments. Not only does it not allow us to experience the person in present time but it creates a barrier that is subliminally or even obviously perceptible to both ourselves and the person who is the recipient of our judgment. By not seeing ourselves in others, we disown aspects of ourselves that manifest in our perception of others.

We relate to each other through our mutual understanding of the human experience. We have a collective mind that takes into account all the minute and diverse variations in viewpoints of all people on the planet. It evolves as the population changes and it includes influences from those who have passed on as well as influences from the potential future of our collective imagination.

This psychic soup creates the ambiance of the world we live in. The future is created by collective intention and the emotional flavor of the times. The more connected we are to higher self awareness by being present with our experiences and recognizing ourselves in others, the brighter the future appears and the more wonderful and amazing our experiences are today. Next time you find yourself passing judgment on someone, thank him or her in your mind for showing you this part of your psyche that you are unwilling to acknowledge in yourself. Feel into that aspect until you can recognize it in yourself. Own the feeling. Greater empathy and compassion are guaranteed if you will do this.

Usually when people begin doing this they will not feel comfortable. Notice how the word "comfortable" breaks down into the words "able" and "comfort". When we disown fragments of ourselves by judging others, we are saying we are not "able" to experience "comfort" while experiencing the quality we are judging. We are "not comfortable with that". Instead of feeling into the source of our discomfort we simply disown it by making a judgment that hardens into a rock solid belief we live by.

The underlying message of the judgment is "not I". The judgment makes us feel better for a while until our world becomes more and more filled with "not I" perceptions. We spend so much time identifying what we think we are not that we forget who we are. We become so disconnected we have lost our place in the world. We feel isolated, cut off from others, cut off from ourselves and most certainly cut off from our spiritual natures. This is the price of judgment. The only way to stop doing it is to first recognize that you *are* doing it. Start noticing when you make a judgment and then just stop! Try this for a while and see what happens.

Is it difficult to let go? If it is, then there is still more judgment to recognize. Ask yourself what is so important about holding that judgment. Keep going until you have an insight about what's really driving you.

Light always casts a shadow and the faster one runs toward the light, the faster one is pursued by the shadow. You cannot visualize it away. You cannot affirm it away. You cannot even transcend it without first facing it head on. Feel your way into the shadows darkening your heart. At first it may not be easy to see what is there but it will become easier as you adjust to the level of light. Discover the truth that lies there. Embrace it for what it has to teach you.

The concept of Satan is the suppression of our darkness, not the darkness itself. Darkness is an aspect of existence we have denied within ourselves. The idea of Satan evolved when we needed something to blame our darkness on because we did not have acceptance for it. The idea of Satan is a collective mind externalization of our disowned fragments, an illusion many of us continue to create. If we all loved ourselves completely, including our darkness, there would not be hostility in the world. Love yourself first, including your darkness, then you will not be scrambling and competing to get others to do it for you. If you do not love yourself, no one else can ever love you enough.

When we call out for help in a spiritual sense, as in prayer, we are calling out to a larger aspect of the collective mind that can help us. The more we appeal to this larger aspect, the more in touch with, and at one with it we become. Prayer is communion with The One.

Our own physical bodies are microcosms of this kind of unity. When we become injured or ill the cells of our bodies rally and call out for help from the larger organism of which they are a part. Adrenalin, blood platelets, repair proteins, white blood cells, T-killer cells, macrophages, whatever is required are supplied to the areas in need. We don't always know what will come and do not have to think about it consciously. Yet these resources of the body are available if needed, through the unifying body wisdom of the larger organism. By the same token, the collective mind is available to help solve problems for us in ways we might never conceive of on an individual basis.

A human being is a miniature version of the universe. Call it a micro-verse. We contain infinite resources for soul evolution and physical healing. Diseased cells are reflections of unharmonious, disembodied soul fragments that exist in the world around us and in the astral realms. These fragments have some form of awareness and like everything else, are aspects of The One. They are discarded emotional fragments of individuals and of the collective mind drifting through the psychic soup of our collective mind. Eventually they may find resolution. Others continue to experience their tormented patterns by being attracted to a person with similar damaging thought patterns. This is sometimes called "negative influence".

Malignant cells are like pockets of terrorism. They proliferate rapidly and in unexpected places, creating fear and dread in the person experiencing them. Fear can only exist in the absence of love. Terrorists, both in the physical world and in the emotional astral realm, are full of fear. They empower themselves by creating fear outside themselves. Their power becomes addictive, because it cannot be sustained without creating further terror. There is no real power because love is not present. Healing all of these conditions requires a radical shift of attention. These influences can and are called into being by our habitual thought processes and daily activities, whether we are conscious of them or not.

The astral realm is the medium of our collective emotional bodies, simmering fragments of un-integrated collective experience as well as emotions in process. It both contains and permeates our beings as it wafts through the universe like an atmospheric condition. The raw voices of happiness, sorrow, love, pain, fear, anger, ecstasy, rage, bliss, terror and sheer madness swirl like a primordial soup, echoing through our existence as a planetary species. The thoughts, beliefs and judgments we hold present most consistently shape the reality we find ourselves in by generating astral forms that hint at possibilities for experiences soon to be created. These astral forms are reflections of our feelings and judgments about any and all aspects of existence we are aware of. Any clairvoyant or shaman will tell you that illness and healing both reveal themselves on the astral plane before they manifest in the body. Held consistently over time, attitudes focus our attention, attracting the flow of reality we now experience.

Destructive emotions that are held over long periods of time generate a magnetic draw toward disowned emotional fragments of a similar nature in the astral realm. To emphasize the unwholesomeness of their nature I refer to them simply as soul fragments.

These soul fragments are disowned or abandoned emotions. They are attracted by people who open the door by exhibiting a pattern the fragment can resonate with, such as an addictive behavior, fear of abandonment or destructive emotional pattern. These are the repetitive voices we sometimes hear in our heads.

If you've felt your way deep into an emotion that continues to repeat itself you either haven't delved deeply enough or it is a soul fragment that you have attracted. If you have willingly allowed your feelings and yet it clings tenaciously, you must firmly take charge. Not in a hateful or resentful way – you don't want to send your disowned emotional debris back into the cosmic soup. But you must firmly make a commitment to your well-being by telling those feelings in no uncertain terms that they must leave you alone. Wish them well but do not allow them to run your life. There is no need to listen to problematic self-talk.

You can do this in a number of ways. State your intention out loud, with finality. If you like personal ceremony you can create a setting for spiritual cleansing, command the soul fragment to go and pray for its integration with The One. Hypnosis can also be very helpful. You may want to seek the aid of a competent trained hypnotherapist or spiritual counselor.

Another way to release the unwanted influence of soul fragments is to gather with others of spiritual like-mindedness. Group gatherings that employ the technique of laying on of hands in combination with focused prayer are very powerful. If you are inclined you may request the services of a member of the clergy. The power of working with others who are aligned in their intention can be greatly beneficial for you. Make sure you are working with people who can maintain a clear and centered space. Otherwise you run the risk of attracting as many soul fragments as you release, or of simply exchanging them.

If you choose to use ceremony, you may want to find some like-minded people who share your interest in doing this. The setting created by the group may be a formal religious ritual or it may be more spontaneous.

Many years ago I participated in sweat lodge ceremonies, based on some Native American spiritual traditions, and found them to be a potent way to help let go of resistant emotional baggage and soul fragments using the power of a group. The ones I participated in usually had about fifteen or twenty people and were held after dark near a large bonfire. The fire was used to heat six or seven hefty river rocks. After they had become red-hot they were brought into the pit inside the sweat lodge at regular intervals and sprinkled with water for steam. The sweat lodge itself was constructed in a particular way out of green aspen boughs, brush and animal skins. Each person completely disrobed and was "smudged" with a purifying smoke of sage, lavender and sweet grass that was wafted around the body before entering the lodge.

Assistants to the ceremonial leader stood by to facilitate the coordination of getting people purified and into the sweat lodge and moving the hot rocks as needed during the ceremony. The leader facilitated the group by leading in chants, songs and prayers. The extreme heat and humidity, the pitch darkness and the sound of water sizzling on hot rocks at the center of the sweat lodge induced a highly altered state of consciousness. The intention of purification was magnified by the intentions of the group, which sat in a circle around the pit containing the hot rocks. Each person stated his or her prayer of intention in turn. After about forty-five minutes the ceremony was concluded and the participants quietly moved to the outside and got dressed, gradually returning to an ordinary state of consciousness next to the bonfire under the starry night sky.

This was primitive but powerful. Releasing soul fragments through ceremony should not be confused as a way to bypass disowned feelings. Ceremony can also be an accelerative tool for the recovery of these disowned feelings. I found that after one of these ceremonies, new emotional baggage would usually surface within a few days for me to explore. It took me a while to realize that my pleas to the universe to grow spiritually were being answered by an increasing awareness of my emotional baggage.

If you decide to use ceremony as a personal growth tool, it is critical to your success that you do not feel blame toward anyone or anything, including soul fragments. Ultimately they are not separate from you.

One of the fastest and most available ways to integrate our disowned emotions and the soul fragments they attract is to begin to breathe more deeply. Are you aware of your breathing? This may sound silly because we breathe all the time or we die. Most of us habitually breathe quite unconsciously, and in a shallow manner. If we find ourselves in a tense situation we may find it hard to breathe. Then when some kind of resolution occurs we take a deep breath and heave a sigh of relief. That is breath integrating an experience. We do it all the time. With the exception of a mother in childbirth, we don't usually utilize the power inherent in choosing to breathe deeply and fully.

Most of us are unaware of how much emotional integration we could accomplish if we would make the effort to breathe more deeply, consistently. One way is to plan to do it deliberately at specific times. I first became aware of this in the 1980's while exploring a process called re-birthing. It was essentially a breathing exercise in which I was instructed to breathe continuously one full and deep breath after another without pause or hesitation. A session usually lasted thirty minutes to an hour.

A facilitator stayed with me to insure I would "remember to breathe" when I hit a wall. The first time I hit a wall it was about ten minutes into my first re-birthing session. It was a block that felt so insurmountable I felt unable to continue. With the facilitator reminding me to "keep breathing" I pushed past it and got my second wind. I felt as if I could continue indefinitely. My mind fluttered with dream-like images and memories and my mouth was filled with a bizarre taste that I couldn't recognize but that seemed distantly familiar. The thumbs of both my hands clenched involuntarily against the first two fingers, a reaction I was later told jokingly is called the "re-birther's salute". Sometimes I would suddenly pause, unaware I had stopped, as my mind evaporated into in a less defined state. As the session progressed, the deep full breaths became rapid shallow breaths but I continued on. At some point there was a feeling of completion accompanied by a sensation of clear quiet space. I felt as though I was floating or as though my body no longer existed.

After several sessions of doing this with a facilitator, I became comfortable doing the re-birthing on my own. Sometimes my partner, Skip, and I would do it at the same time or get together with other re-birthers and do it as a group. The session was over when the last person had stopped the rhythmic breathing and all had lain quietly for a while. Then we would discuss our experiences.

Sometimes I would do the re-birthing and feel little emotion during the process, but a day or two later, or even longer, I would experience an emotional pattern with an "in your face" intensity that demanded integration. Repression was no longer an option. I found the best way to examine the pattern was to dive right into the center of the feeling. The dream I described in the chapter *Finding the Shortest Path Home* tried to communicate that to me many times before I finally got it.

Although I haven't done re-birthing in years, I still feel it can be a valuable tool to awaken the inner fire of Spirit. When I did re-birthing on a weekly basis, I noticed that colors appeared brighter and all my senses felt heightened.

Over the years I've developed a breathing exercise of my own that has delivered powerful experiences. I lie flat on my back in bed and take a full deep breath, letting it out comfortably and naturally until I feel empty. I don't force the exhalation. I take my next breath when I feel ready but it does not have to be immediate. It is important only that each and every breath is full and deep all the way to my abdomen. There are no shallow breaths in between the full and deep ones. The breathing is not rushed but it is deliberate and deep. The inhalations are drawn to full capacity and the exhalations are relaxed. I do this for thirty to forty-five minutes, sometimes longer. It seems to draw in tremendous amounts of life force, as I always feel more aware, energized and charismatic afterward. Colors are brighter. Realizations are spontaneous and profound. Occasionally I've had sessions that resulted in the feeling of being out of my body.

One time I did this exercise while staying in a hotel. It caused me to shift into an awareness that I can only describe as detached and observational. It was as though I existed before time and creation. When a sound in the room brought me out of quiet timeless space I experienced it as profound. For example, a toilet leaking water one drop at a time in the bathroom was recognized by me as drops of condensation from the heavens falling onto a primordial creation pool harboring the first amoebic life forms. At the same time I felt myself existing as the amoebic life forms I was also observing. It was fascinating, both having the experience and watching it at the same time.

Later the same night, still doing the breathing, I felt as though I was drifting through the astral realms, again as a detached observer. I could sense the presence of millions of soul fragments, which I recognized as un-integrated aspects of the collective mind. They floated gently and randomly through the ethers, their combined voices a low chorus of moans, each awaiting a time when it might be invited or allowed into the realm of human experience. In fact, this experience gave me many of the concepts I have described about soul fragments. Deliberate breathing is extremely powerful and should never be overlooked as a tool for integration of the emotional body.

In the beginning it may not be easy to discern between your un-integrated emotions and discarded soul fragments of the collective mind, so do not be quick to play the victim and blame everything on the collective mind. That will only re-affirm your powerlessness. Own what is yours, what you have created through the filters of your personal judgments. You must start by beginning to feel everything you've resisted feeling for as long as you can remember. Does that sound scary and forbidding? Remember, the shortest path to where you want to go - inner peace - is the one you've been avoiding. You will find that although it leads through uncharted territory it isn't as far to your destination as you may think.

When a person takes responsibility for the state of his life, from the minutiae of everyday living to the condition of the world he perceives around himself, and if that person is able to fully experience his own participation in the creation of that world, the astral realm becomes a little clearer and the collective mind becomes a bit more integrated in its path toward wholeness.

You may be afraid that once you start to feel your unwanted feelings you may never be able to stop. That is a common fear. So when you start and it feels like the feeling goes on forever, go into the feeling that it never ends and see what happens. It is sure to provide insights for you. These insights are pearls of enlightenment to form a strand that will encircle your entire being with the wisdom of self-knowledge, the bliss of inner peace.

We have all experienced everything,
And we are experiencing everything, at any given moment.
The great web of collective mind
Vibrates with the intentions of every soul;
It informs and affects the state of the world.
Intentions ricochet in chaotic confusion,
And find order creating the wonder of experience.
We all do the best we know how.

22

Collective Mind

Everything each person thinks and feels becomes part of the collective experience and affects the collective mind. You are not separate from the whole. You cannot be. Your agreement to be here in this earthly incarnation is to evolve spiritually by means of the human experience and through that experience to contribute to the evolution of the collective soul in its journey back to The One.

The more we interact with each other and allow the recognition of ourselves in the behaviors of others, the more rapidly we evolve toward perfection as a species. Interaction with other human beings is a necessary aspect of spiritual evolution. While it is important to retreat periodically from others to meditate, pray and integrate one's experiences, the need to interact as little as possible with others, or perhaps a chosen few, is a resistance to experiencing certain feelings that arise when doing so. There is a difference between being comfortable with solitude and needing to retreat continually from others.

Life is all about learning through experience. It is teeming with a richness that begs to be explored. This is why we have five physical senses, minds and emotions. We also have non-physical senses that connect us to our super-conscious spiritual natures and to the collective mind. When a person is really in touch with his spiritual nature, intuition guides choices. Beliefs are created purposefully rather than as a result of conditioning. Life feels full of possibility. The physical senses and emotional body experience the realities created by our minds and spirits. Feeling these experiences keeps us in touch with our higher selves. The conduit from spiritual to physical is a flow of feeling. In its highest manifestation it is an open channel that flows both directions.

The recognition of our oneness is described in many ways: the moment of truth, Nirvana, inner peace, Samadhi, the Kingdom of Heaven, transcendence or communion with God. It is the re-birth of Spirit. It is a life-changing experience that can only be experienced in the present moment. The moment you realize you are there, you are not. But even an instant is enough to remember your essence, your magnificent grandness, what some have called your glory in God.

An eternity of wisdom can be recognized instantly in the right moment. It is infinite knowledge that has no words to express what it is. The scribes of spiritual masters could only write about it through the filters of their limited understanding, challenged even more by their inability to experience what they were writing about, a state that by its nature has no words to describe it. So as dutifully as they tried to convey the wisdom of the great power they sensed in their spiritual masters, their writings are usually interpreted by those who do not have the "eyes to see" the truth behind the words nor the "ears to hear" it. Some intuitively understand this oneness without having experienced it for themselves. They feel the message behind the words or they feel the presence of the spiritual master who spoke them. Trust in their feelings gives them faith.

The extended and more aware aspects of ourselves, our higher selves, coordinate creative orchestrations within the scope of a larger aspect of The One. In the big picture our Spirits do not see themselves as separate from each other or from The One. They have created separation only as a means to experience the wonder and profundity of differentiation. Individualized aspects of The One (what we think of as our personal Heart-Soul-Body-Mind identities) are the keepers of our souls while we are incarnate. We, the keepers, interact and co-create with each other to produce the backdrop we call life.

During an incarnation we learn through the medium of experience. Each soul-keeper makes choices through free will, changing the way something is experienced at any time through the power of decision. The thoughts and acts of a person have a profound effect on the quality of life experience that person has. Those same thoughts and deeds influence the collective at another level. Like a pool of water, if a drop is added there is a small splash where it lands. The water nearest the drop is most affected, but the movement can be detected with gradually lessening effects at depths and distances far from the place it landed. Although not completely visible, the entire pond is affected by the movement of the one drop.

You may wonder how you can be the source of all you perceive when there are others in the world with you. Your perceptions are your own. No one else has quite the same slant on the world as you do. Although others may appear to have the same point of view on many ideas, those points of view are colored by their own judgments and dispositions, filtered by experience.

Individual realities are created by your perceptions based on past experiences, both in this and previous incarnations. Individual realities begin as choices made by the soul while disincarnate to present real life lessons to itself when it returns to the amnesic physical realm. Our personal realities become more complicated as choices made by free will cause us to interpret and experience the results of our choices.

These realities are created by our beliefs and prejudices. They are shared by others in a complex web of interactions with the larger reality shared by the collective mind, which in turn is contained within an even larger domain of consciousness. Moving outward into the universe and beyond are forms of consciousness unrecognizable to our limited perceptions. This larger domain includes angels, spirit guides, nature spirits (fairies and elves), disincarnate beings, demonic soul fragments and ascended spiritual masters existing in dimensions outside of time and space. It also includes any other form of consciousness imaginable in any dimension either imaginable or unimaginable.

Aspects of our shared world reality are created by the collective mind of the planet. For example, as recently as six hundred years ago, most people in the world believed the world was flat. They lived their lives according to that belief, afraid that if they ventured far from home, they would fall off the edge into a great unknown. They experienced the world as flat because that was their belief, based on their perceptions. It took someone with a fresh perspective to point out another possibility, and the collective mind was forever changed.

If great numbers of people shift toward a more spiritual awareness while incarnate at the same time, this will certainly affect the collective soul of the planet.

As the spiral of individual consciousness expands to include more it becomes less defined. Any attempt to define The One, which includes all manifestations in and out of the universe, as well as all things unmanifest (the Void), limits the ubiquitousness of its nature. When our higher self – Spirit – plans a life for us to experience, it creates a special combination of viewpoints, a one-of-a-kind being with a uniquely different life. Its experiences are at all times subject to the exercise of free will by the person experiencing them. Choices are made to resist an experience or move into it. We choose to believe what we are taught or to be open to see other possibilities.

Choices determine the course of our lives and the quality of our experiences. Free will is an experiment of The One in its decision to experience physical reality. It is the source of our lifeline to the divine as well as the source of our estrangement from it.

The journey toward spiritual wholeness begins within the heart of each person who awakens to the realization that the way he has been living life has not produced real and deep satisfaction. Since this would not occur without the necessary earth experiences to awaken the realization, the journey toward spiritual wholeness really began at the moment you decided to incarnate as a separate and distinct aspect of The One. This would include journeys into other realms or dimensions of experience in which you existed as something completely unimaginable by space and time earth definitions.

Lifetimes of adventure, boredom, pain, suffering, happiness, despair, hopefulness and every other experience you can name have brought you where you are today. At some level we all understand the desire to be a tyrant. We all know the humility of being a peasant or beggar, as well as the glory of nobility. Because time is a creation of the mind and our collective human species is a continuum of consciousness, each of us has an awareness of all of these experiences, whether or not we have experienced them personally for ourselves. Because of our shared connection to The One we experience it all. It is part of our group experience and our collective mind. It is what allows us to feel empathy for another human being.

Another way to think of the collective mind is by using technology as a metaphor. The human mind is like a computer. I'm sure you've heard that before. Taking that idea further, this computer has a wireless connection to all other computers (minds) on the planet. Some of the files are hidden (privately held beliefs and judgments) and some are openly shared by the entire network (collective mind beliefs such as the concepts of gravity, space or time). The integrity and strength of the network is based on all computers having clear communication with the modem which accesses the server (Spirit conduit to The One). If you think of planetary consciousness as a complex wireless network that shares information, you begin to understand the importance of seeing yourself in others. Everything you do, say or think has some effect on the worldwide wireless network of collective mind.

Nothing demonstrates this better than examples from disastrous events. In 2004 Hurricane Ivan made landfall at the area I live in as a strong category three storm. Its arrival at the peak of high tide made the resulting storm surge incredible by previous benchmarks. Many people were killed. Over three hundred homes in our local area were completed destroyed by the surging flood and thousands of others were damaged by fallen trees and blowing debris. I felt sad and depressed for a couple of weeks after the storm, even though our home was one of the lucky ones that did not have extensive property damage. The intensity and scope of the devastation threw a blanket of sadness over the entire area. It was palpable to all who lived here. Just seeing the Red Cross truck in my neighborhood made me burst into tears. I was experiencing the pain and loss of many through the wireless network of our local collective mind.

Later in the year, when Malaysia and Thailand were inundated by a deadly tsunami killing hundreds of thousands, the sense of loss was felt deeply around the world. Thousands rallied to bring aid, both in the form of money and supplies. Many helped with their presence in person, on location.

In 2005 Hurricane Katrina came ashore at New Orleans and Mississippi. The scope of damage was unprecedented compared to previous tropical storms in the States, due to the huge numbers of people affected by the damage, displaced from their homes and the unsanitary conditions left in its wake from excessive flooding. As the country and even the world watched in shocked amazement, even those of us who had gone through several other terrible hurricanes shook our heads in sorrow.

When terrorists hijacked planes and attacked the United States on September 11, 2001, people who lived nowhere near the affected areas and who had no relatives or acquaintances living there were nonetheless deeply moved and disturbed by the events. We experienced a collective sadness and depression as a nation while we grieved for the loss of so many. Emotions and judgments transferred wirelessly across thousands of miles of land and sea to re-shape our collective outlook and modern world. The collective mind of the world has not been the same since.

We are all connected like a large web. Our consciousness allows us individual expression and free will, but our unity causes all aspects of consciousness to be affected to some degree by the choices of all other aspects.

Some of us still cannot identify with anyone outside our own individualized expressions of self. It may be too much to ask you to identify with the consciousness of, for example, a terrorist. If so, at least begin where you can. See yourself in your perception of those in your immediate world who aggravate or annoy you in some way. Make it a daily habit. Find someone in your life that makes you feel uncomfortable in some way and begin to explore what it would feel like to be that person. Take note of any insights. Doing this leads to compassion for everyone in the world.

As you get better at it, move on to more challenging personalities, then expand to explore various ethnic groups. Explore the group consciousness of individual ethnic groups from whatever point of view you bring to them. Feel into them. Do this until you feel compassion for them. Everyone in your world is your mirror.

The wireless network of collective mind underlies all human interaction. It is often said that communication is ten percent verbal and ninety percent nonverbal – or some similar ratio. A lot of the nonverbal part is body language and posturing, voice tone, facial expression and so forth.

There is also a very important and often overlooked aspect of nonverbal communication and that is our intention. If you think by keeping your thoughts to yourself that they will be contained, or that having selfish motives won't matter as long as you don't express them, you are naively mistaken. Others pick up on our intentions, even if only subliminally. I don't mean to say we can read the thoughts of another verbatim. It is a transference of feeling. Often, the feeling of the other person is not a coherent thought that can be deciphered verbally. But we are all familiar with what is commonly called a "gut feeling". When we communicate there is a sense of the other person. Do you know how you sometimes just immediately trust someone, or conversely, "get a bad feeling" about someone? That is part of the nonverbal communication and it operates on a frequency outside the rational mind. It is part of the wireless network we are all tuned in to. I would venture to say it is a much larger contribution to the overall communication process than most researchers have even begun to recognize.

For example, you may be carrying on an animated conversation with someone, all the while thinking how impressively you are making your point, how aware you are of the positioning of your body and voice tone and how convincing your argument is while maintaining a non-threatening posture. And all the other person is getting out of it is "Wow, he's really full of himself." She hasn't heard a thing you've said. I am going out on a limb here. I believe the inner chaos of subconscious intention and self-consciousness contributes as much as fifty percent or more to the communication of one person face-to-face with another.

With so many people in the world unhappy with themselves or their lives, work or family situation, is it any wonder our world is filled with conflict? We are too ready to criticize, disagree with and make wrong "the others", whoever those others may be in our self-created universes. We may hope to feel better about ourselves in this sad attempt. There is an old saying, "Whenever you point a finger at someone there are three pointing back." Remember this next time you feel critical. If you can recognize it as a symptom of your own feelings of guilt or unworthiness you have noticed something very important. Ask yourself, "What have I not forgiven myself for?"

The most common collectively resisted emotion is hate, and yet there seems to be more of it in the world every day. We want to believe we are only full of love and light. We believe hate is not part of us. We believe it is out there in the world, but not within our own hearts. If we feel hate, even for a moment, we quickly attempt to transform it into another feeling, or hide the feeling so deep inside that no one will ever see it, including ourselves. Some people are so convinced that thinking only positive thoughts will change the world that they project all their hatred onto others, as if there really were any "others" to project it upon. By disowning their own hate, they hope to change the world. It can't happen that way. These same people are baffled when terrorists come out of nowhere, manifesting all the disowned hatred in the world. Then they say, "The terrorists are evil and full of hate - I am not like that". Meanwhile they hate the terrorists but feel their hatred is justified. As a society part of the collective mind plans to seek them out and destroy them, hoping to eliminate fear and hate from our lives. Deep inside each and every one of us knows intuitively that this will never eliminate fear and hate. You can't eliminate hate with more hate!

The challenge for collective mind is for each person to individually embrace his or her own hatred. What or who is it that really gets to you? Embrace the feeling and explore it. What are you afraid of? Explore the depth and quality of it. It is not pretty. When you allow yourself to sincerely own it you will be amazed and humbled. It will be a revelation. Only then will you be able to let it go.

Many years ago I got in touch with my own hate and allowed myself to feel deeply into it. I was completely ashamed and humiliated, even though I had not shared the feelings with anyone else. In the privacy of my bedroom I cried into my pillow in hateful rage. At the same time I hated the feeling of hate. It was a malignant mass of blocked emotion begging for release. I was amazed at the depth of it, the solidity of its substance, the violent urges it contained and the power of it to overwhelm me with shame and self-loathing. It was not necessary to act out anything in the physical world. The experience was completely internal. Nothing I have ever done has taught me more humility and compassion for the perceived faults of others.

We fear hate because we are afraid if we give into it, it will win. We are afraid of its depth and intensity, afraid it will overpower the broken fragments of love in our hearts we cling to. The truth is, until we acknowledge our hate it has already won. It controls us through fear, judgment and terrorism in the world. It does not allow the peace of a loving heart. The "dark night of the soul" is the rite of passage through our fear, hatred and doubt that allows us to experience the ecstasy of love and the peace of wisdom that lies on the other side.

I tell you this so you will not feel alone. If I can endure the scandalous shame I felt while exploring my own darkness and come out of it a better person, so can you. You can be a happier, more tolerant person than you ever thought possible. You can learn to find peace in the present moment. As you learn to experience with more presence and less judgment, you will discover the turbulence in your heart settling down. The sense of doing things becomes more timeless. Life becomes an active meditation. The surrender of your judgments does not feel like you are giving up anything at all.

I see the big picture now.

I hear the one word.

I smell the breath of the divine.

I taste the nectar of the gods.

I feel the power of presence.

I know I am The One,

And The One is also me.

I am all of it,

And it is all of me.

23

Returning to The One

The world hangs in a fragile balance. As we move toward a more planetary consciousness, the most fragmented aspects of our collective mind have re-asserted themselves with disruptive tenacity. Communication and technology have brought nations of the world together as never before in a more global economy with a global identity. Violence and war have a long tradition. Terrorism, the newest "enemy", is more fragmented and less obvious than past enemies. The enemy is no longer "out there" but mingles within our societies, disguising itself and finding shelter wherever it can, often enjoying the fruits of a system it conjures to destroy. We have discovered that it is very difficult to locate terrorists.

Nevertheless, each person is holy. The judgments we have as individuals and collective groups about other persons and groups in the world that we consider to be evil or spiritually inferior keep humanity in the chaos of conflict. We must embrace our hate individually, and on a massive scale, in order to let go of it. Until we do the human race will continue to fear terrorism and feel hatred as part of its collective experience. We are as responsible for the terrorism in the world by our denials and self-righteousness as the terrorists are for acting out hatred within the collective mind.

The most sinister expression of Spirit is an aspect of The One. You may believe the terrorists in the world today are separate from you. They are separate only in the sense they are choosing to act out an aspect of existence that you have chosen not to. The evil and suffering in the world are opportunities for us to wake up and seek a way back home, to The One. Those who manifest evil are attempting to relieve their own suffering. All suffering is a result of separation from The One. Denial of the evil that exists in the hearts of people who choose not to manifest it leads to further suffering, because separation from The One is strengthened. The fact that a person will not act them out in this lifetime does not mean that evil thoughts or violent urges have not occurred to him. We all contain the potential to hate and harm; we make our choices through free will.

Terrorists have elevated their hatred to religious status. Because terrorists believe what they are doing is right, they have no shame of hatred and violence. They are willing to act it out. What they have denied is their love. They have grown up in the absence of love. They do not realize that love is the source of ultimate power. They know power only through the creation of terror in the world around them. Their craving for power can never be satiated. It is an addiction that can only be healed by the presence of love. They are pitiful in their lack of true power, attempting to gain it by casting a blanket of fear over the world. Their egotistic assertions of the importance of their cause belie the sense of worthlessness felt by the individuals supporting it.

See them for what they are: un-integrated fragments of our collective mind. The terrorists have been disowned by those living in fear of them, who think of them as "not I". The terrorists are willing to embody the hate, prejudice, righteous anger and rage we are all capable of feeling. We have projected those feelings out into the world so we don't think we own them. They have literally come back to haunt us. They are the extreme condensation of destructive thought habits disowned by so many that they have solidified into a very self-defeating thought pattern of the collective mind. To beings coming from a perspective that see themselves as peaceful and loving, they are a disowned fragment of the collective soul, unloved and resisted.

The way to de-fuse this explosive projection is to re-own the hateful fragments lurking in our own subconscious minds, one human being at a time. It is the source of ultimate power, a power which does not seek to dominate because it permeates all. Get in touch with your own hatred and feelings of powerlessness.

Healing the collective mind begins with an inner decision to do it by each individual. That is where we must start. We must all, each and every one, find ways to integrate the hateful, manipulative, intimidating aspects of our own personalities. Doing this on a personal level helps the entire planetary species. We must appreciate the terrorism for what it has shown us about ourselves so we may feel compassion for those fragmented beings who act out the darkened places in our own souls. If you can do this, you have begun to do your part to change the collective attitudes that keep these scenarios in place. Maybe everyone won't join you just yet but you will have found a way to experience a quiet pool somewhere along the edge of a roaring river.

Is this possible? It is one of many possibilities. Will it happen? Maybe, maybe not. Until we get in touch with our hate, we will continue to be unable to feel the purity of unconditional love. Compassion eludes us, either coming from us or directed toward us. It is a mind-boggling paradox that getting in touch with your ability to hate will allow you to experience greater compassion than you ever thought possible. It does not mean you will continue to hate. By allowing the hateful feelings you have hidden for years to bubble to the surface of your awareness, you give them the freedom to pop and float gently down the river of life, integrated into its current. This is the power of non-judgment.

If you believe you have no such darkness, if you refuse to acknowledge the evidence that is already in front of you in the form of terrorism, you continue to perpetuate the horror. It is a lot to swallow. We have been spitting it back out for eons.

All of creation is a manifestation of The One. Why would The One create the kind of bifurcation we are experiencing? It is a desire to experience the fullness of its power, the diversity of its creative potential, the unlimited possibilities it contains and ultimately to re-discover itself in the amazement and gratitude of reconciliation.

We are a civilization in process. We are evolving to a higher state of consciousness gradually, almost imperceptibly. Not all are ascending at once. It is as if two dimensions of experiential intelligence are co-existing in the same space. The wall between them is at times transparent, at other times opaque.

It's like looking into a pond of water. At first you see only your own reflection but upon further examination you notice life on the other side of the surface. To get past our own reflections we need to look below the surface of them to what lies beneath. Each must accept full responsibility for his or her part in the creation of the world as it is today, the mirror. When the mirror becomes transparent we are able to see through to the other side, to a richer awareness. As we walk through we turn to look back and we discover that the thing causing the reflection has disappeared. We are bathed in the waters of experience and beyond that there is only the clear space of possibility.

Effective Goal Creation – Getting to What You *Do* Want

A great deal of this book has been a discussion of how to let go of what you don't want in your life. Once you've done this for a while, a lot of space opens for something different to occur. This is a quiet space, pregnant with possibility. Although I believe it is extremely beneficial to spend as much time as possible in this space, which I call the Void, it is not practical or feasible to stay there all the time. No matter how euphoric or at peace you may feel in its silence, eventually you are going to feel the desire to create something new.

It is the nature of being physically alive to do, to experience. It is the nature of Spirit to be, to exist in a limitless state. To observe with awareness the experience of life is the union of heart, mind, Spirit and body. It is the mission of life. It is the still small voice within that calls us to remember who we are.

In order to create experiences that support the mission of your higher self, it is imperative that you first clear the debris from your personal landscape, as we have discussed in this book. Next, it is important to set clear goals for yourself so that you do not continue to live your life through default.

If you give away your creative power by denying its existence in your life or by not recognizing the spark of the divine that ignites your very existence, other aspects of the collective mind will gladly seize the opportunity to use it to their advantage. The more you turn your power away, the more out of control your life feels and the more powerless you become.

This is the way many people go through life. They feel like victims. They believe nothing that happens to them is their fault. They believe God or the universe is testing them. And on and on. People who think this way simply don't want to take responsibility for the things they don't like in their lives. They are overwhelmed by their sense of unworthiness, which they believe is real. They would rather continue to judge others and place blame than to feel the vulnerability that lies below the lack of self-worth. They would rather feel self-righteously indignant than examine the contents of their hearts.

I know since you have come this far with me you sense the possibilities for great things in your life. You are ready to own your magnificence. And I believe in you. It's time to create some worthy goals.

A lot has been written about goal-setting, and its importance has become more widely recognized in recent years as a tool to help achieve what a person wants from life. Today, there are hundreds of information products available at widely varying costs that outline processes for effective goal setting. Basically I believe they can all be distilled into these simple steps:

Make a list of all the things you want to have or experience in life. Be specific and set times for their accomplishment. The more specific the information you give the creative power within you, the better the result will be. Make your list in a special journal or pad that you can easily have at hand and devote it entirely to this purpose.

Pick out your top ten and number them in order of their importance *to you*. Then re-write your top-ten list in order of importance.

Read your list at least three times a day, at different times of the day. Read it out loud at least once a day.

Think about what you want as often as possible. It is important not to analyze how your goals will be accomplished, particularly if you are reaching further than you have dared to in the past. If you feel very confident about reaching them, you are not aiming high enough.

Associate with people who have some of the things you now want. If some of them are people you can't meet personally, buy their books or products, or use their services.

These steps will awaken the power of your reticular activator. This is the attractor force of your subconscious mind. It's something like casting a gigantic net into the ocean of possibility. The bait is your attention to the desired outcomes. This great power within you will begin to attract situations, circumstances and people that will miraculously unfold to you the means to the accomplishment of your goals. This process can be very subtle, particularly over time. Although this may seem like a passive step, it is important to be alert for these seemingly coincidental opportunities and act on them.

Maintain the vision. As goals are achieved or become unimportant to you, feel free to revise the list as you see fit.

Although your list may start out somewhat superficially, many worthwhile desires will eventually find their place on your list. As you unfold into the awareness of your ability to create what you really want, your desire to live in integrity and compassion will increase. One desire will be to help others as you have been helped. Ultimately, everyone's life mission is to improve their existence. A natural result of accomplishing this is a desire to help others to do the same.

Express gratefulness to the Universe – and to the part of your creative self that has allowed you to manifest what is important to you. A grateful heart is blessed with more and more reasons to be grateful.

Awanestika.

How I came to be known as Moonstone

Many people ask me how I got the name "Moonstone". "Were your parents hippies?" or "Is it Native American?" are the two questions most often asked. The name "Moonstone" came as a gift to me.

In the late 1980's I participated in a small workshop retreat for self-recovery, where we were each given a different name, the purpose of which was to help us move out of our old conditioning. We tend to have a whole repertoire of attitudes we correspond to our birth names. Using a different name during the retreat was a tool to help us relate to ourselves in a new way, with a fresh perspective.

To avoid taking on attitudes associated with other names we might be familiar with, we were given unusual names that corresponded to one of the five elements of Chinese medicine, namely earth, fire, wood, water and metal. Other participants had names like "Lightning" (fire), "Mountain" (earth), "Ripple" (water), "Cypress" (wood), or

"Tin" (metal). "Moonstone" was an earth name. I loved it immediately.

At one point during the retreat I discovered that my true feelings had been totally numbed out. It came up for me when, during a deep breathing relaxation exercise, I saw and felt nothing while others seemed to be seeing mental movies of incidents in their lives that helped them understand how they had become as they were. It was a pattern for me that I often felt nothing or fell asleep during a meditation or visualization and I felt very frustrated. My facilitator pointed out that numbing out *is* a valid emotion and it had worked for me when I was young to avoid feeling more pain than I was willing to show or feel. It had become a lifelong habit.

At that retreat I came to realize that my feelings had been hardened, as if petrified into stone. The emotional body, which lies in our energy fields just outside the physical body, had developed a hard, protective armoring. The moon has been symbolic of emotions in many earth-based spiritual traditions. We have ups and downs according to the phases of the moon. A proportionately higher number of crimes and accidents happen during periods when the moon is full – ask someone who works in the police department or ER. The ocean's tides, affected by the moon's phases, are of the element water, and water is also correlated to the emotional body in earth-based traditions. To me the name "Moonstone" came to symbolize my recognition of emotions being turned to stone, not flowing like water anymore. Later it also came to symbolize the union of heaven (moon) and earth (stone) to me. Today it is a constant reminder that I am Spirit incarnate. The gift of that name is one that I treasure. I've been Moonstone ever since. A year later, when I knew it was going to stick, I changed my name legally. It is a symbol of my re-birth, growth and ever-unfolding awareness, as well as a reminder of from where I have come.

Ten years later I added "White", the surname of my life partner, Skip. "Star" is from the tarot card tradition of self-knowledge. The Star card is associated with my astrological sun sign, Aquarius. It symbolizes one who is a way-shower, shining light on the path of Spirit. Although I no longer use astrology or tarot for guidance as I once did, I still find them interesting, particularly with regards to their archetypal imagery.

With Gratitude

Iwant to express my gratitude to both my mother and my late father. Their deep love for each other has been a model by which I have gauged my own relationships. When I was a child, they trained me with firmness, discipline and a sense of responsibility, yet always within an atmosphere of love and forgiveness. When it was time for me to find my own way, they gracefully stepped aside and allowed me to discover life on my own terms. They may not have always agreed with or liked my choices but they were always ready to listen, always interested in another point of view and always accepting of me with whatever version of reality I brought to the table. For me, this has been their greatest gift.

I also wish to acknowledge the many friends, co-workers and chance acquaintances I've known or met along the way who have contributed in some way to my current experience of the world. You are my teachers. Many have touched my life with their presence. Some have offered me challenges and others have offered me strength and support. I am grateful for both. There is not room to name everyone here but for anyone who ever knew me, either deeply or in passing, know that I am speaking directly to you with thankful appreciation.

I am profoundly grateful for the help and support that has come to me from many directions during the production of this book.

Last, I am grateful to The One, source and essence of all that is and is not, for the gift of free will and for the amazement of experience.

REFERENCES

The Doors of Perception and Heaven and Hell by Aldous Huxley, Harper Colophon Books, Harper & Rowe, Publishers, New York, 1963.

Walden by Henry David Thoreau, first published in 1854, published since through various publishers.

Leaves of Grass by Walt Whitman, first published in 1855, published since through various publishers.

Spring Forest Qi Gong Personal Learning Course by Chunyi Lin, Learning Strategies Corporation, Minnetonka, MN, 2000.

Genius Code Personal Learning Course by Paul R. Scheele and Win Wenger, Learning Strategies Corporation, Minnetonka, MN, 2002.

Between Heaven and Earth, A Guide to Chinese Medicine by Harriet Beinfield, L.Ac. and Efrem Korngolf, L.Ac, O.M.D., Ballantine Books, a division of Random House, New York, 1991.

Alice's Adventures in Wonderland by Lewis Carroll, first published in 1865, published since through various publishers.

Be Here Now by Baba Ram Dass (formerly Dr. Richard Alpert, Ph.D), Lama Foundation 1971, San Cristobal, NM; Hanuman Foundation 1978, 23rd printing by Modern Press, Albuquerque, NM, 1979.

Holy Bible – King James and New International Versions.

INDEX

ORDER INFORMATION

If you found this book meaningful and would like to share
its message, you may use this order form to receive copies
shipped directly from the publisher.
Make a photocopy and fax this form to:
Spirit Wind Publishing
Fax: (850) 936-8384

In the U.S. order toll free:
1-877-832-4400
Or call: (850) 515-1416

E-mail orders to: admin@spiritwindpublishing.com.
Be sure to provide all information below.

Order online: www.spiritwindpublishing.com

Full Name

_____

Shipping Address

_____

City, State, Postal Code

_____

Country

_____

Phone: _____
(In case we need to call about your order)

E-mail address:

_____

Price per book:
>1 book - $23.95
>2-4 books – 10% discount
>5-10 books – 20% discount
>11-15 books – 30% discount
>16-20 books – 40% discount

Call or e-mail for quote on larger quantities

Number of books ordered: _____ **Sub-total: $** _____
6.5% sales tax for books shipped to
Florida addresses: $ _____

Shipping:
>For 10 or fewer books:
>U.S. $5 for the first book, $2.25 for each
>>additional book.
>
>For 11-20 books: U.S. $2.25 per book
>   **Shipping total: $** _____

International orders: Call or e-mail for shipping quote.

Order total: $ _____

_____ Check enclosed (payment must be in United States currency)

_____ Use my credit card: _____ Visa _____ MasterCard

Card number: _____

Expiration date: _____

3-Digit security code on back of card: _____